A YEAR IN MotoGP

A YEAR IN

Published by Virgin Books 2008

10 9 8 7 6 5 4 3 2 1

Copyright © James Toseland 2008

James Toseland has asserted his right under the Copyright, Designs
and Patents Act 1988 to be identified as the author of this work

Photography © Gold & Goose

First published in Great Britain in 2008 by
Virgin Books
Random House, 20 Vauxhall Bridge Road, London SW1V 2SA

www.virginbooks.com
www.rbooks.co.uk

Addresses for companies within The Random House Group Limited can
be found at: www.randomhouse.co.uk/offices.htm

The Random House Group Limited Reg. No. 954009

A CIP catalogue record for this book is available from the British Library

ISBN 9781905264469

The Random House Group Limited supports The Forest
Stewardship Council [FSC], the leading international forest certification
organisation. All our titles that are printed on Greenpeace approved
FSC certified paper carry the FSC logo. Our paper procurement policy
can be found at www.rbooks.co.uk/environment

Mixed Sources
Product group from well-managed
forests and other controlled sources
www.fsc.org   Cert no. TT-COC-2139
© 1996 Forest Stewardship Council
FSC

Designed by Peter Ward

Printed and bound by Firmengruppe APPL
Aprinta Druck, Wemding, Germany

CONTENTS

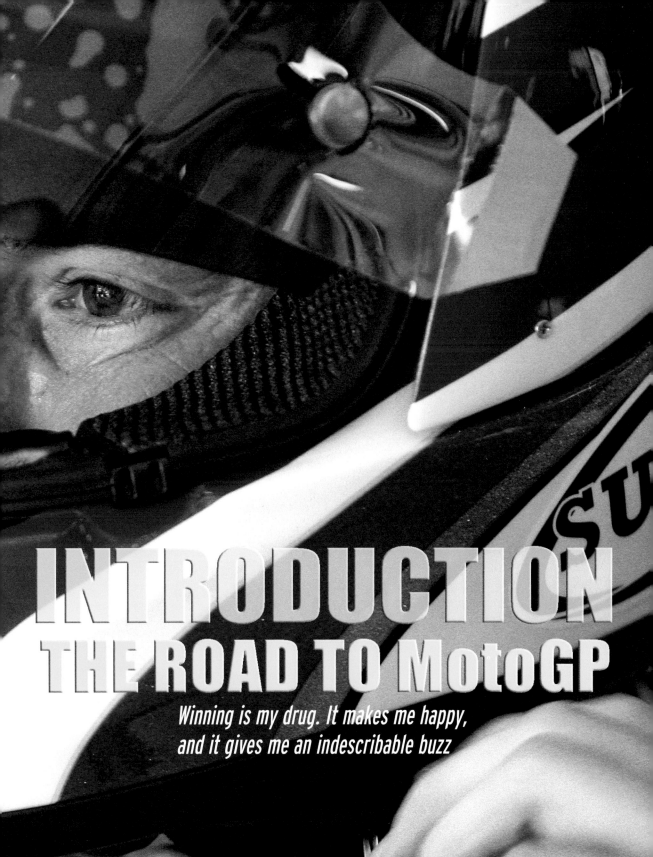

INTRODUCTION
THE ROAD TO MotoGP

*Winning is my drug. It makes me happy,
and it gives me an indescribable buzz*

▶ The podium at Brands Hatch, 2007. The best racing day of my life so far.

Pushing myself to reach new heights has always been important to me, and has become almost second nature. And not just in my racing career – even when I was really young, when I took up the piano I was determined to master playing it really well.

So, early on in 2007, even before I had clinched the World Superbike championship for the second time, when my manager Roger Burnett and I discussed the possibilities and pitfalls of my switching from WSB to MotoGP for the 2008 season, I couldn't wait for our plan to come to fruition.

Sure, it was a gamble – and there were many people, including good friends, who saw it as such and wondered if I was doing the right thing, leaving my comfort zone. From my point of view, I didn't have a split-second of doubt.

I had enjoyed being in WSB. Who wouldn't revel in being a winner and a champion? Winning is my drug. It makes me happy, and it gives me an indescribable buzz. But even battling and beating great competitors like the Troys – Bayliss and Corser – Noriyuki Haga and Max Biaggi stopped me short of my ultimate dream to be the best among the best. And that meant the elite class: MotoGP, the pinnacle.

Moving to MotoGP was a gamble and many people wondered if I was doing the right thing

I knew it would be tough. But I had seen enough of the action on TV to confirm my belief that taking on super-gifted guys like Valentino Rossi and the rest of them would be a challenge to relish and a test of my own resolve and skill where I most wanted it. But the bike and the team had to be good, otherwise I would be wasting my time. That's when I put my future firmly in Roger Burnett's extremely capable hands and left all the wheeling, dealing and sorting out a team to him.

Honda would probably have made me the highest-paid rider in WSB history if I'd opted to stay in that class, but money was not my driving force and it was easy to resist its lure once I'd convinced myself that MotoGP would give me the best opportunity to realise my ambition of being ranked alongside riders and great champions like Mike Hailwood and Barry Sheene. Once the idea was firmly fixed in my head there was not a moment's thought about turning back.

It wouldn't be fair to say that I didn't have anything left to prove in WSB. Clearly, with Carl Fogarty as four-times world champion, and at that point me having won it only once, there were still challenges to be faced and a job to finish.

But I got everything strongly on track in 2007 and dominated the championship from the word go, despite Biaggi winning the first leg of the first race with me taking the second leg. Roger said from that point it was obvious to him that I was going to be the man to beat – and we began to think that, if I won the 2007 title the only thing I could do in 2008 was win it again. Anything less would have been a step backwards, a devaluation of myself as an individual and as a competitive rider.

I made the early decision that I wanted to go to MotoGP, so Roger and I sat down and concluded that it should only happen if we could get a competitive team and a competitive bike, a potential winner, with a competitive tyre.

The criteria for a competitive ride, a good bike, had to have the 2008 stamp on it, a factory entity. The tyre had to be either Michelin or Bridgestone. The team had to answer my needs in terms of how I like an outfit to operate, rather than how good it is, and the way I could fit in. I do really well in a friendly, family-type atmosphere.

Honda would probably have made me the highest-paid rider in WSB history if I'd stayed, but money was not my driving force

I was happy to leave all the background work to Roger while I concentrated on trying to clinch the WSB championship again

Roger flew to Jerez, Spain, for the first European round of MotoGP and talked to just about every team – Suzuki, Kawasaki and Ducati. Repsol Honda was a closed shop, a no-goer, because we knew their riders had ongoing agreements and, anyway, historically they never took on a rookie.

It was the Yamaha situation that was the most interesting. And that, Roger decided, was where the best opportunity lay for me.

Roger came back armed with information and evaluated it himself. He drew up a table of all the riders, the teams, their strengths and weaknesses, and did it quite systematically and statistically. It all added up to one finite point: Yamaha was, in his opinion, the best option, *if* he could get me into a team.

I was happy to leave all the background work to Roger while I concentrated on trying to clinch the WSB championship again.

Once the idea to move to MotoGP was firmly fixed in my head there was not a moment's thought about turning back

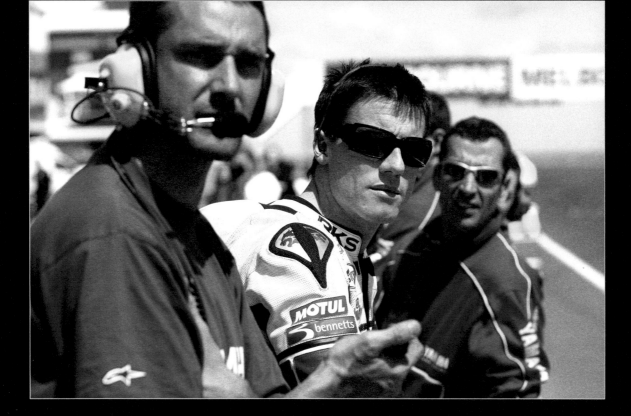

▲ It became clear to Roger that Yamaha really wanted me.

Roger figured that Yamaha may have had a final year to run with Rossi – we will have to wait and see what does happen – and that 2008 was maybe going to be the Italian's last year with them. The writing was on the wall that Casey Stoner and Ducati were a real threat – after the domination of Honda and Yamaha in the blue riband class Ducati came along and reshuffled the pack slightly. But, as far as Roger was concerned, it seemed wiser to follow the historically laid path and stick to the old, tried and well-trusted manufacturers from the Land of the Rising Sun. They knew how to win races and championships. It was in their pedigree.

However, I was already on a Honda with the excellent Ten Kate team from Holland – but they obviously wanted me to stay where I was in World Superbikes. I could see it from their point of view as it would be difficult for them to find a replacement for me, but I was determined that I deserved a chance to go to MotoGP with a full factory bike, as my obvious ability demanded.

Anyway, at that time Honda were not performing particularly well, so it was a negative situation. The other interesting aspect, I learned from Roger afterwards, was that all the people who wanted me to stay with Honda and remain in WSB wanted to talk to me and not Roger. He felt he was not liked, but squeezing him out turned out to be an oversight on their part.

All Roger wanted to do was what was best for me. He was the guy in a position to evaluate the outlook and the prospects, whatever effect – good, bad or indifferent – it had on Honda. It was his job. They thought they could by-pass him by talking directly to me. But I was content to leave it all to Roger.

Yamaha were in a position where they needed to come up with something really strong for 2008, as much as anything to persuade Rossi they were on the ball to keep him beyond his contract period. That was their objective. Roger knew they would be working their socks off over the winter and that is why Yamaha fitted his evaluation and became the target.

They had a secret meeting, all the top Yamaha brass and Roger, at Donington Park at the British Grand Prix, and it became crystal clear to him that they really wanted me. Roger had made them well aware of my skill as a rider, my strengths and appeal as a highly promotable figure. They knew from my battles with Nori Haga, their WSB hope, just what a tough rider I could be. They appreciated, too, that someone like me,

who is generally perceived as a nice guy, can be just as ferociously committed as the so-called bad boys. My whole image fitted their requirements.

And, better yet, the team boss of the Tech 3 outfit, the extremely charming and likeable Herve Poncharal, was a long-term friend of Roger's from his Grand Prix race days, a quality guy well regarded in the paddock, and just the right sort of character to bring me along in my new role.

Herve said later he could not believe his luck when the deal was all signed and delivered and I, a rider he had long admired, was to be in his team. And when Roger looked inside the set-up at Donington Park and, from the pitwall, watched them operate, he knew he had chosen wisely. The promise from Yamaha HQ was that the relationship between Tech 3 and them was going to be even stronger.

I gained valuable experience latching onto and following lads like Rossi, Stoner and my new teammate Colin Edwards

Other teams briefly in the frame, and discounted for various reasons, had viewed me as too much of a risk. Kawasaki had the attitude: Who is James Toseland? Other line-ups, like Paul Denning's Suzuki team, preferred not to take a chance on a MotoGP rookie, even though I was a WSB champion heading for a second title, and a determined competitor. Livio Suppo at Ducati was desperate to sign me for the satellite Dantin line-up, where we'd had experience before, but we couldn't see that it was going to be any benefit.

It took a little while longer to nail an offer together and it was only when Roger had done the deal, and listened and believed the promises of upcoming benefits and improvements to the bike, that he let me in on the arrangements. The process of elimination he had followed left us where we wanted to be in the first place, on a Yamaha – and we sprang the news at a get-together at The Ivy in London. To say the assembled guests, mainly media, were staggered is an understatement.

I know Ten Kate were terribly disappointed. But it was no disloyalty on my part. I had enjoyed every minute spent with the team, on and off the track. And I regarded them as firm friends as well as excellent and professional performers. In the final analysis I think they understood my motives to move on were based on a genuine desire to mix it with the world's greatest riders in MotoGP. Of course, they were devastated, shocked in fact, but eventually they gave me their blessing. They knew I had given them my all when I was carrying their colours.

I was determined that the announcement of my switch to MotoGP was not going to allow me to take my eye off the ball

Next up was Brands Hatch, the biggest event of the year for me, with the championship finely poised, a title to be firmed up and a massive partisan crowd to be entertained and given something special to cheer. I did just that – I was so fired up it was frightening – with a memorable double. I was determined that the announcement of my switch was not going to allow me to take my eye off the ball or forget and forsake my dream to win the championship for a second time, and the sell-out Brands Hatch weekend was to be my showcase . . . in more ways than one. From a specially set-up stage on the start-finish line I played keyboards and sang the national anthem for the 100,000 fans. And they loved it. They loved it even more when I romped home to a double. I regarded that achievement as one of the greatest and most satisfying of my career. In practical and numerical terms it virtually clinched the title – I opened up a massive 66 point lead over Nori Haga.

I regarded the achievement of winning at Brands Hatch as one of the greatest and most satisfying of my career

It's history now that I went onto win the title – and Ten Kate were brilliant, they gave me permission to test for Yamaha before I had wrapped up my contract with them and sponsors HannSpree. And, as a thank-you farewell, I performed for the team at an end-of-season party in Haarlem, Holland.

Roger first broke the news of the MotoGP deal to me at Brno, in the Czech Republic, the race before Brands Hatch. He flew in early, Thursday, and we were sitting in my motor home when he said he didn't want to fill my head with any unnecessary trivia ahead of the weekend, but did I want to know how his talks had gone? I was dead calm and put the kettle on and made a cup of tea – then told Roger he should just tell me which garage to go into for my first MotoGP test!

Dorna, organisers of MotoGP, had been desperate for years to have a British rider, and a successful one, make the breakthrough. They realised the massive following it would create for their UK market. Even the BBC was desperate to support the idea of a top British rider – and, after I had signed for Yamaha, with the hope we might have, at long last, a British world champion in the elite class to cheer, they extended their TV contract until 2013.

All in all, the move was reckoned to be ideal. Only Honda were not happy. And Roger took a lot of flak because he had been the prime mover and organiser, but only in my best interests with my tacit approval.

The best riders in the world, and a formidable line-up for the 2008 MotoGP season.

The bottom line is that Roger did a fantastic job in getting me into the sort of team, Tech 3 Yamaha, that put me back into a comfort zone while, at the same time, filling me with confidence that their intentions matched mine in terms of where they wanted to figure in the championship chase. I could not have wished for a better boss than Herve Poncharal. His experience, his attitude, his ability to make me feel right at home straight away, even before I had even sat on one of his bikes, were crucial factors that all served to confirm Roger's judgement on which team I should join.

Mind you, I didn't get off to the best of starts. At the first test in Sepang, Malaysia, in November I dropped the bike. And I was only six laps into the new phase of my career! I was following my teammate Colin Edwards and lost the front end – I got too much lean angle on the Michelin and off I tumbled. But by the end of the day I was pretty pleased with myself: I was lapping just 1.5 seconds off Casey Stoner's lap record.

Stepping off a WSB bike onto a MotoGP, with 800bhp under me, was a real eye-opener. And I realised I was on a learning curve with a whole set of new techniques to be mastered.

One of the most difficult aspects was the difference in the stopping distance. The Yamaha took a lot more physical strength in braking, and even though I had worked hard at my fitness, I was totally knackered by the end of the session. What with that

The floodlights of
Qatar make a spectacular
backdrop to the start of
the new season.

and me hitting the anchors 25 metres short, and people rushing by on the brakes, I got an early wake-up call. I realised I had to forget as quickly as possible all I had learned in Superbikes and to focus hard on the differences, and difficulties, I now faced in MotoGP on the Yamaha M1. The engineers were great in playing their part and patiently filling me in on what I really needed to know about the Yamaha's behaviour.

At each of the following test days I got more and more used to what to expect and how to maximise on the Yamaha's performance. I also gained valuable experience latching onto and following lads like Rossi, Stoner and my new teammate Colin Edwards, who was only too happy to help out and share his performance data as much as he could and to boost my confidence even further by saying how impressed he was with my debut. It was all of this that gave me towering reassurance that I had made the right move.

To say I was itching to get started in the season proper was probably the understatement of the decade. Roll on Qatar, a track I know well and where I have been a winner.

WELCOME
QATAR

*To say I was itching to get started
in the season proper was probably the
understatement of the decade*

QATAR

Losail Circuit, Doha, 9 March

'James has done a fantastic job. I was impressed with the way he performed - so it is hats off to him.'

CASEY STONER

*Until I got down
to the real business
on the track, no
amount of verbal
backing was going to
help my natural anxiety*

Whatever doubts I'd had about my ability to compete on equal terms with the established and experienced guys in MotoGP disappeared rapidly under the floodlights of Qatar in the crucial build-up to my race debut a week later.

I'll admit I was worried about how I would fare amongst riders who were regarded as the finest and fastest in the world, but who wouldn't be anxious in my position? I was the new boy gazing on a grid featuring class acts and champions like Casey Stoner and Valentino Rossi, supported by an all-star cast of the best of the rest. My two World Superbike championships counted for nothing now. They were history, consigned to my CV.

The encouragement I was given by my manager Roger Burnett and a whole host of supportive friends and family members was welcome; but I knew instinctively that, however uplifting the words, until I got down to the real business on the track, and proved myself in the company I craved to keep, no amount of verbal backing was going to help my natural anxiety.

I never dreamed, however, that the test session prior to the curtain-raiser race would turn out to be such a confidence booster. I was careful not to let it turn into an ego trip, but it did confirm to me that I was most certainly not around to make up the numbers. My confidence was shared and echoed by my Tech 3 team boss, Herve Poncharal, and my teammate, Colin Edwards.

To say I kicked off to a flying start is an understatement. I got to within minutes of finishing the Qatar late-night run-out as the fastest rider, and was only topped on the time sheet by Yamaha rider Jorge Lorenzo, the double world 250cc champion, who had moved up to the top ranks as the session drew to a close.

I could hardly believe it, but what a boost for the upcoming race. My best was 1m54.592 – with only Lorenzo ahead of me on 1m54.522. Behind us were Randy de Puniet (1m54.873), Colin Edwards (1m55.464), Casey Stoner (1m55.330), Andrea Dovizioso (1m55.550), Nicky Hayden (1m55.674), Chris Vermeulen (1m56.119), Alex de Angelis (1m56.249), Valentino Rossi (1m56.256) and Loris Capirossi (1m56.450).

I was really delighted to be holding my own against the full-works riders. My time on a qualifying Michelin tyre beat Rossi's 2007 pole position by 0.5 seconds. What a lift!

I had been really apprehensive after making the switch from WSB. After all, guys like Neil Hodgson and Carl Fogarty – both great and unbeatable world champions in WSB – and Shane Byrne and Chris Walker – all fine and talented riders and tough competitors – had given it a go without the sort of success they sought hard to achieve. Why should I prove to be any different?

◄ ▲ I couldn't have wished for a better test session

I knew my strengths on a production bike, but a full-blown prototype with all its upgraded and quirky characteristics, handling, braking, cornering and acceleration was a dramatically different proposition. And yet here I was, fronting the action and being given nothing by anybody except, now, some respect. It was my definite aim to carry it through one week later to the first-ever MotoGP under lights.

The best aspect for me was that on my long run I was extremely consistent. There was only 0.8 seconds between my best and my worst lap, and that's a satisfying range. But it was unbelievable how much power I had to cut.

Despite a severe tyre chatter throughout the entire three-day test, I had been tenth at my first MotoGP outing in Sepang in November 2007, and I looked on in awe as Nicky Hayden clocked an incredible time. I remember thinking, I'm not sure I can do this. But then I recalled it was like that when I first ran superbikes. At the time, I wondered how the hell Troy Bayliss and Colin Edwards could turn in such fantastic and regular times. I used to think, Am I going to be able match that?

But I listened and watched and learned, just as I did ahead of Qatar. And I let my confidence have its head even though the bike was well down on the speed of those of Rossi and Stoner.

see him win a race, I really would' CARL FOGARTY

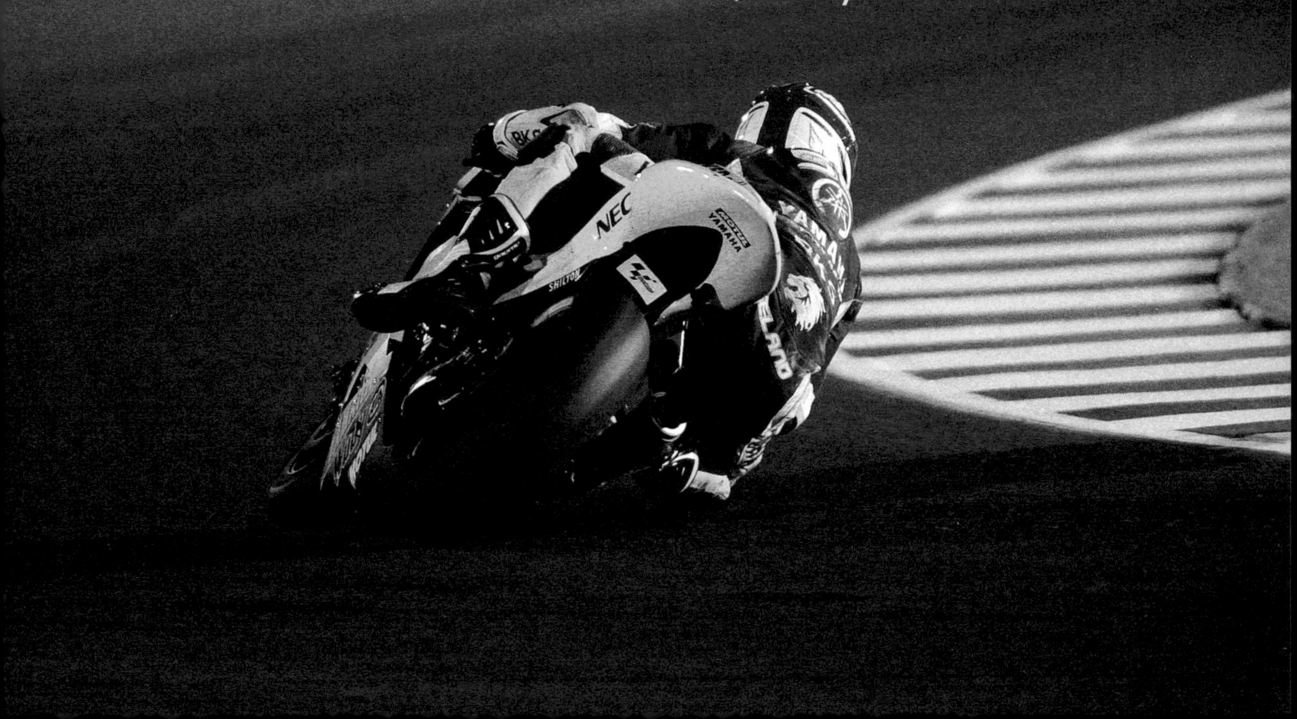

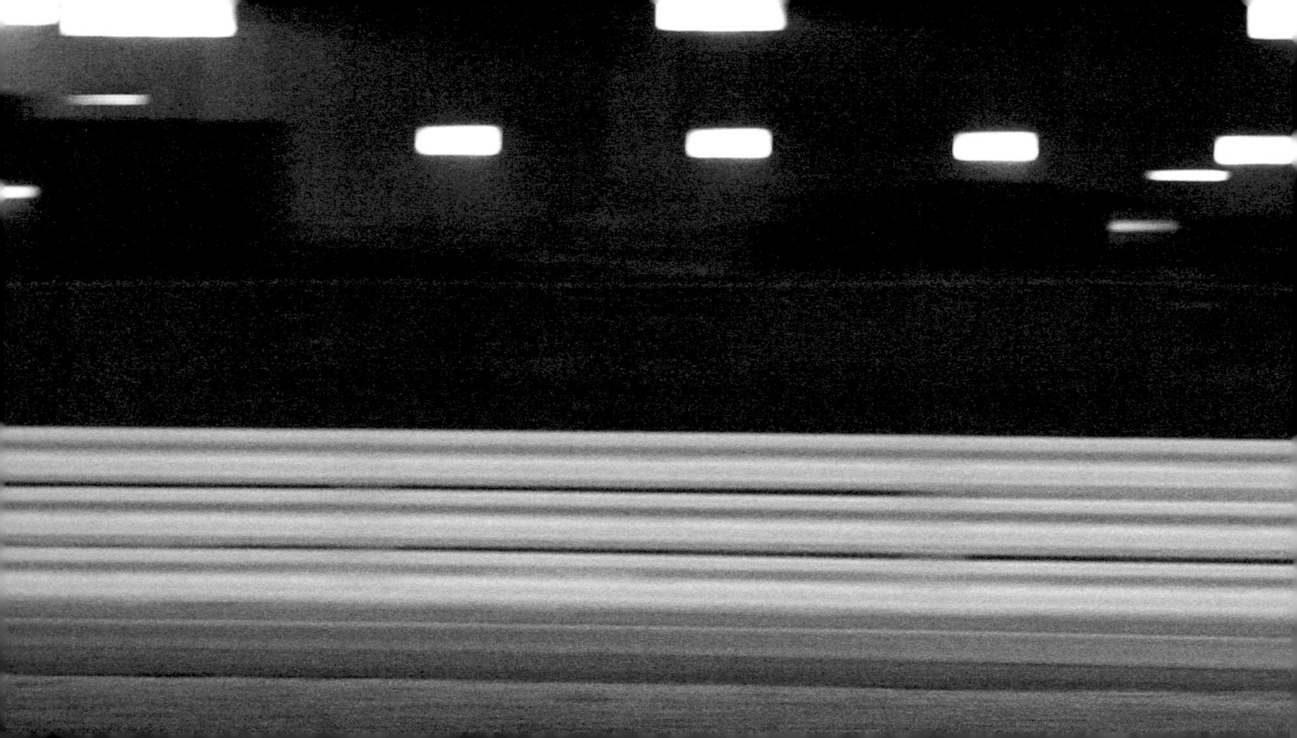

he is even faster. He is riding very well and can do a great job this year, so many congratulations to him.'

I didn't expect, however, that I was about to have such a close-fought battle with Rossi, on the more updated and uprated Yamaha, in a race that was just about the toughest of my career.

My preparation was as intense and painstakingly planned as ever. But this time around there was one significant difference . . .

I had honed myself as well as I could in the gym in the close season and I felt fitter at 27 than I had ever been. But there was still another crucial step to take: I wanted to ensure that the night race, with an 11 p.m. start, did not catch me out.

'For me Toseland is a big surprise.
He was fast in Sepang and Jerez
and now in Qatar he is even faster'
VALENTINO ROSSI

*I was really happy with my start.
I made sure I was as aggressive as I
could be, without being dangerous*

After the test I stayed on in Qatar and turned my days upside down. I exercised in the gym at midnight, had juicy steaks at 2 a.m., and went to bed about 5 a.m. I didn't get up until noon, and then had a breakfast. People at the hotel thought I was some sort of freak. And when Roger Burnett flew in to keep an eye on me, and I hustled him off to the gym and then for a big late, late supper, he too was convinced I had lost it. But it paid off and when race day came my body was totally adjusted to the well-after-dark start. I don't know if any of the other guys followed the same regime, but I wanted to guarantee that I was fresh and well suited for the unusual demands of a race near midnight under floodlights and in humidity that would otherwise have been draining. As it turned out, I finished the race, a real hard one, barely breaking sweat. And what an eye-opener it turned out to be . . .

I was really happy with my start, my first-ever in MotoGP. I made sure I was as aggressive as I could be, without being dangerous, in order to make my mark and my presence felt as quickly as possible among guys who raced hard and yielded nothing without a fight.

I got away quickly, but braked late for turn one and nearly went off. Luckily I just missed Dani Pedrosa's back-end and cut back in to third place. And that wasn't too bad at all.

In turn two – and by now I had settled in nicely – I dived under Jorge when he didn't exit too well, but the grunt of his bike brought him back into play. We came together in a bit of a dodgy moment. Jorge shoved his bike across my front end just as I was lined up for a pass, but he left the door open a tiny bit and I went for it.

After that I trailed Rossi and Dovizioso and tried all I could to overtake, but it was too tricky a situation and the risks would not have been worth taking – I could well have crashed out trying too hard on a bike that was down on power compared to theirs.

I rode just about the hardest race of my career for sixth place, hanging onto Rossi's coattail but unable to topple him as I really wanted to. I came within split seconds of beating him and was right on his back wheel for the last eight laps. It would have made my day if I'd been able to beat him – but I reasoned I would get another chance soon, when I would be on better machinery and a little more used to the action in MotoGP, as well as having learned more about the habits of top guys like Valentino and Casey.

I rode just about the hardest race of my career, hanging onto Rossi's coattail but unable to topple him

LOSAIL INTERNATIONAL CIRCUIT

WELCOME

23:15

LAP

1 52

2 1

3 48

4 46

5 5

6 65

At the start I was bursting with confidence, having clinched second place on the grid in qualifying. And a close encounter of the paint-swapping kind with pole-setter Jorge Lorenzo, when I barged by him, gave me another lift – but I could not hold onto the advantage. My YZR-M1 was yards slower than the bikes of the other likely front runners and it didn't take long for me to be overtaken and relegated. I peaked at 200.32mph with Rossi's factory-engined Yamaha hitting 202.69mph and Marco Melandri's Ducati GP8 topping out at 207.78mph, the quickest of us all.

What I lacked in speed, though, I had to make up with some really tough and uncompromising riding. I desperately wanted the pneumatic valve motor that Rossi had, but was told I would have to wait for the third round in Estoril, the scene of the Portuguese Grand Prix, before I could get one. Otherwise, I reckon I could have been in with a firm chance of a podium finish. And that was also the opinion of a good number of onlookers. What a breakthrough that would have been.

As it was, my sixth place was afterwards widely hailed as a triumphant start to my MotoGP career: I certainly exercised a good deal of patience and vowed not to do anything that would jeopardise or compromise my very satisfactory progress, or risk the wrath of Roger Burnett! Though the first lap was as hairy as it gets.

When you've had a career full of wins and podiums, as I had in WSB, your initial thought is, 'Oh, God, no. Sixth!' But when I had cooled down I took a more rational look at my debut performance, and I realised how well I had done. I had qualified on the front row, finished in the top six and had not been dropped off or overwhelmed by Rossi, and I reckoned I had shown what I was capable of achieving, even on a bike that was down on power.

I guess I could have had a go at taking on Rossi and Dovizioso – they were clocking similar lap times to mine and were locked in a tremendous scrap – but I decided that the risk was not worth it. They were dropping me off four bike lengths down the straight, even though I got it back into the corners. Then they'd be gone again. My best hope was that one of them would make a mistake and leave me a gap.

But imagine if I'd dived under Valentino while he was concentrating on Andrea's threat, and had wiped him out. That would have triggered a massive hero-to-zero plunge. I wasn't prepared to take that chance, however tempting. I just patiently enjoyed a close-up of the action being played out only a few metres ahead of me.

*My overall conclusion was a conviction
that I could compete with the best*

Pos	Pts	No	Rider	Nation	Team	Bike	Total time
1	25	1	Casey Stoner	AUS	Ducati Marlboro Team	Ducati	42'36.587
2	20	48	Jorge Lorenzo	SPA	Fiat Yamaha Team	Yamaha	42'41.910
3	16	2	Dani Pedrosa	SPA	Repsol Honda Team	Honda	42'47.187
4	13	4	Andrea Dovizioso	ITA	JiR Team Scot MotoGP	Honda	42'49.875
5	11	46	Valentino Rossi	ITA	Fiat Yamaha Team	Yamaha	42'49.892
6	10	52	James Toseland	GBR	Tech 3 Yamaha	Yamaha	42'50.627
7	9	5	Colin Edwards	USA	Tech 3 Yamaha	Yamaha	42'51.737
8	8	64	Loris Capirossi	ITA	Rizla Suzuki MotoGP	Suzuki	43'09.092
9	7	14	Randy de Puniet	FRA	LCR Honda MotoGP	Honda	43'09'590
10	6	69	Nicky Hayden	USA	Repsol Honda Team	Honda	43'14.941
11	5	33	Marco Melandri	ITA	Ducati Marlboro Team	Ducati	43'20.871
12	4	21	John Hopkins	USA	Kawasaki Racing Team	Kawasaki	43'26.444
13	3	56	Shinya Nakano	JPN	San Carlo Honda Gresini	Honda	43'26.458
14	2	24	Toni Elias	SPA	Alice Team	Ducati	43'35.119
15	1	50	Sylvain Guintoli	FRA	Alice Team	Ducati	43'35.517
16	–	13	Anthony West	AUS	Kawasaki Racing Team	Kawasaki	43'42.230
17	–	7	Chris Vermeulen	AUS	Rizla Suzuki MotoGP	Suzuki	43'11.483
			Not classified				
		15	Alex de Angelis	RSM	San Carlo Honda Gresini	Honda	31'26.773

When I climbed off the bike after what was an eye-opener of a first MotoGP race for me, I felt I had found my niche. I certainly did not feel out of place or outclassed in anything, except the lack of pace of the bike, and was only 3.5 seconds off a podium finish.

My overall conclusion, and one I determined to carry forward throughout the season, was a conviction that I could compete with the best. I was comfortable, I didn't scare myself, I didn't stick my neck out and I didn't overdo it or find myself trapped into any acts of recklessness. I only do this very hairy and risky job for a living, and have only made the sacrifices I have, in order to be a winner. It's the way I am, the way I think – it's my belief and my priority in life. And I can't begin to explain the phenomenal boost to my morale that my first outing among the most talented riders on the planet gave me.

Casey Stoner, the winner of the race and the 2007 champion, was generous in his appraisal of my arrival on a scene he had so significantly dominated, when he said after the race, 'Coming from Superbikes, which required a completely different riding style, James has done a fantastic job. I was impressed with the way he performed to get a sixth place – so it is hats off to him.'

Roll on Jerez . . .

SPAIN

Jerez, 30 March

'James was a little bit too aggressive. He touched me twice – and the second one nearly put me off the track.'

LORIS CAPIROSSI

Sometimes I wonder at my own sanity. I must have been crazy to even think of racing the second round in Jerez, having to go to work at nearly 200mph, fight for track space and mix it with a whole horde of fiercely committed riders when I was suffering from a severe attack of bronchitis.

Doctors at the track in Spain wanted to ban me from racing when they saw how ill I was. It was touch and go as I struggled against a 39.2°C temperature, feeling like I needed to sleep a lot more than I needed to race. I stayed in bed the whole of the Thursday before the race, I felt that lousy – really rough and debilitated. But I resisted the doctors' advice that I go to hospital and relied on their medication, pills, jabs and drips to pull me through. And it did the trick, but only just.

I spent more time with Dr Costa in the trackside medical centre than at my motor home. The doctors had to get the OK from the FIM, the sport's ruling body, that the drugs they were pumping into me were cleared by the authorities. They even organised a nurse to come to see me to check my overnight progress. They were that concerned.

I must have been crazy to even think of racing the second round in Jerez

I was still struggling throughout free practice, even though that morning I'd texted Roger at his hotel with the words: 'I'm on it, pal', meaning I was set to go. But I was kidding myself. I was so weakened I fell off in the second session, luckily without injury. I'd got the suspension setting wrong and lost the front end. But it was a wake-up call for me.

The race was a nightmare, my toughest ever, and I barely remember half of it. I was so uncomfortable, hardly able to breathe, coughing and spluttering and terrified that I was going to throw up in my helmet. My concentration was wrecked. My oxygen intake was critically down because I could snatch only half-breaths. But I was determined to carry on and not quit.

I was so weakened I fell off in the second session, luckily without injury

Coming off the bike
during testing was a real
wake-up call.

Sometimes, even when the action was at its closest and toughest, I felt as if I was riding round in circles and looking in on myself. It felt completely unreal. Afterwards, when I sat in the garage and I tried to recall what had happened throughout the 27 laps, I could only remember about half of it.

What carried me through, aside from my natural fitness and strength I guess, was a fired-up, now-or-never resolve not to back down.

I sat on the grid before the start thinking that I didn't want to be watching this race on telly at home tomorrow night, or on a season's review show in November, seeing myself limping across the line down among the also-rans and no-hopers just because I was ill. That would upset and frustrate me and I would be slagging myself off about a missed opportunity.

The race was a nightmare, my toughest ever, and I barely remember half of it

I crossed the line after what I was sure had been about two hours racing and saw my pit board indicating I had 22 laps to go

I kept repeating to myself that, although I may not be feeling 100 per cent – more like bloody awful, in fact – I should grit my teeth, master the discomfort and give my best shot. That way I couldn't blame myself for not putting in a half-decent effort. It took a big slice of willpower to follow through.

I had to dig deep because I was totally empty of energy. But as the race went on, and I got tangled up in a series of spats for fifth, sixth and seventh places, my discomfort was overtaken by an adrenalin surge to get the best out of myself. Long before I got ill, and encouraged and boosted by my strong showing in Qatar, I had hoped that I might grab a podium place in Spain.

As it was, a second sixth place in succession was my reward for a lot of fast and fevered effort and some really closely contested racing, especially into the last couple of corners. I was the first British rider since Niall Mackenzie in 1990 to earn two top-six finishes on the trot.

I had a real battle with Chris Vermeulen, Loris Capirossi and Andrea Dovizioso, right until the last corner, and that kept my mind from wandering into self-pity.

I crossed the line after what I was sure had been about two hours' racing and saw my pit board indicating I had 22 laps to go. After that I ignored all the messages from the pit and got my head down. I passed Vermeulen with six laps to go – and wondered where the hell all the laps had gone.

On the final corner it was all or nothing at all with a madcap scramble. I got squeezed out of fifth place when Dovizioso somehow got underneath me. How he stayed on the track is a mystery that will long puzzle me. I was just tipping the bike into the corner when he belted by like he was still in fourth gear. I got him back – but we touched on the exit. Then Capirossi came by to rob me of fifth place by just 0.4 seconds. It was a mega disappointment, but I was content knowing that under the circumstances I could not have done any better.

I had to dig deep because I was totally empty of energy

I got squeezed out of fifth place when Dovizioso somehow got underneath me

To be in the top six again was where I wanted to be, and the best I could have really hoped for given that the bike was down on grunt and I was feeling physically and mentally wrecked. The result gave me a lot of heart for the races that were to follow, particularly with the promise of the updated motor for Portugal.

Mind you, I was a bit surprised that afterwards the three guys I had been tangling with throughout the race had a pop at my riding style. They accused me of being too aggressive when I fought up from tenth place on the first lap to be mixing it with them into the exciting Curva Sito Pons onto the back straight. I passed all three of them, and that was the only place I could have done it.

I was getting really good drive off the corner, but still couldn't get level on the straight because I was about 5mph slower, and it would have been do or die on the brakes. My front tyre was so good it behaved perfectly and it got me through safely enough to dive under the three of them. I took my chance because I felt confident that I could get by without any risk either to them or me. They didn't see it that way . . .

Vermeulen said later: 'James hit me quite hard and it tore my leathers apart, ripped the handlebar weight out of the bar end and knocked my brake lever up. He rammed into me. Loris said that James hit him, too. And he is probably going to get some of his own medicine back from some of the guys.'

Capirossi shared Vermeulen's view. He said: 'James was a little bit too aggressive. He touched me twice – and the second one nearly put me off the track. But I don't really have a problem.'

And Dovizioso chimed in: 'The move James made was a little too aggressive – maybe he just needs to be more careful in the future.'

My feeling was – and still is – that I did nothing wrong. I was tough, sure, and aggressive because that's the way I compete. I readily accept that if I race that way, giving nothing, yielding to nobody, then it is open to the other guys to race that way too and give me as hard a time as I guarantee to give them. But at the same time it's

Pos	Pts	No	Rider	Nation	Team	Bike	Total time
1	25	2	Dani Pedrosa	SPA	Repsol Honda Team	Honda	45'35.121
2	20	46	Valentino Rossi	ITA	Fiat Yamaha Team	Yamaha	45'38.004
3	16	48	Jorge Lorenzo	SPA	Fiat Yamaha Team	Yamaha	45'39.460
4	13	69	Nicky Hayden	USA	Repsol Honda Team	Honda	45'45.263
5	11	64	Loris Capirossi	ITA	Rizla Suzuki MotoGP	Suzuki	46'02.645
6	10	52	James Toseland	GBR	Tech 3 Yamaha	Yamaha	46'02.929
7	9	21	John Hopkins	USA	Kawasaki Racing Team	Kawasaki	46'03.417
8	8	4	Andrea Dovizioso	ITA	JiR Team Scot MotoGP	Honda	46'03.570
9	7	56	Shinya Nakano	JPN	San Carlo Honda Gresini	Honda	46'07.690
10	6	7	Chris Vermeulen	AUS	Rizla Suzuki MotoGP	Suzuki	46'10.212
11	5	1	Casey Stoner	AUS	Ducati Marlboro Team	Ducati	46'17.344
12	4	33	Marco Melandri	ITA	Ducati Marlboro Team	Ducati	46'19.619
13	3	13	Anthony West	AUS	Kawasaki Racing Team	Kawasaki	46'20.928
14	2	15	Alex de Angelis	RSM	San Carlo Honda Gresini	Honda	46'20.992
15	1	24	Toni Elias	SPA	Alice Team	Ducati	46'44.679
16		50	Sylvain Guintoli	FRA	Alice Team	Ducati	46'49.563
			Not classified				
		5	Colin Edwards	USA	Tech 3 Yamaha	Yamaha	9'10.348
		14	Randy de Puniet	FRA	LCR Honda MotoGP	Honda	3'31.127

important to make sure it is fair and not dirty or recklessly dangerous. This is a deadly and dodgy sport and you have to have good sense and not intend to cause anybody to crash or hurt themselves, while at the same time remembering you are out there to do your best to win.

I am the first to hold my hands up and apologise on track if I've cut somebody up by my error or my over-zealousness – and I expect the same treatment.

Whatever those three felt about any over-aggression was not shared by Paul Butler, the race director and ever-watchful official who monitors every minute of the action and in close-up on his TV screens at race control.

When he heard about the criticisms, which hadn't been aired to him, he said: 'I can confirm that we have received no complaints from any of James's fellow competitors.

'Although we have witnessed James make several forceful passes we have not observed anything that crosses the line into the unfair or dangerous zone.'

And that was good enough for me. It was the green light to keep racing as hard as I know how.

PORTUGAL

Estoril, 13 April

I knew what the bike was capable of and, to be honest, it was capable of better than where I finished on it

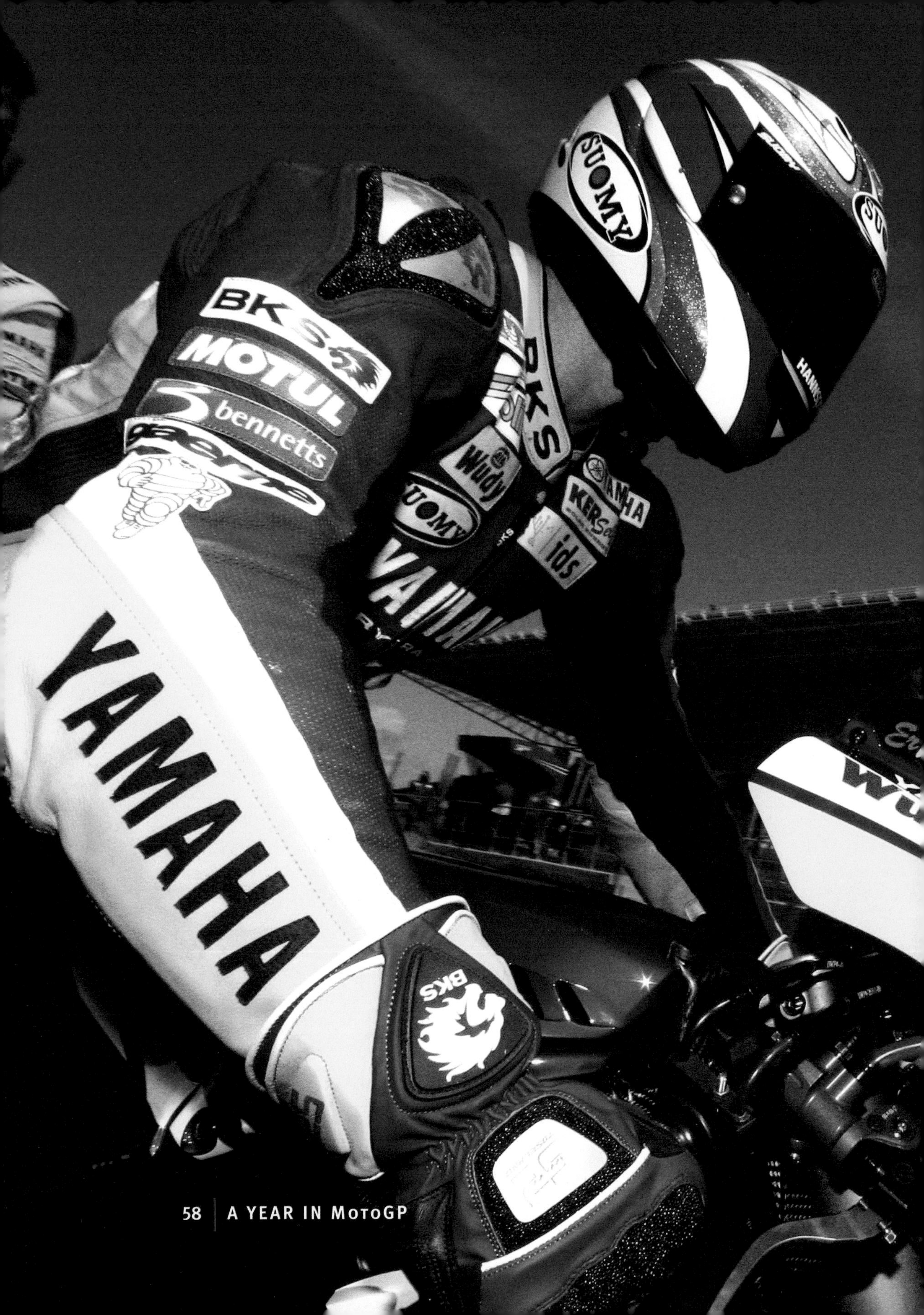
BKS
MOTUL
bennetts
YAMAHA
SUOMY
Wudy
ids

The bike I had for the race in Portugal enjoyed the overdue benefits of the updated pneumatic valve motor – and about five miles an hour extra at the top end.

But in the race things didn't go quite as well as I had planned or expected with the extra power. Rain on my visor at the start upset my concentration and I got bogged down mentally and lost five places on the first lap.

I suppose it must show how well I'd started in MotoGP when I was disappointed with a seventh place finish in only my third race. I reminded myself that I am the rookie and I must not expect too much too soon. But I knew what the bike was capable of and, to be honest, it was capable of better than where I finished on it. My fault, I guess. But I wasn't helped or encouraged by the light rain that fell intermittently throughout the 28 laps.

The more I am around the Tech 3 set-up, the more I am convinced I made the right move

It was, I felt, ironic that just when other guys were pinpointing me as being too aggressive, it was a lack of aggression that cost me dearly in this race. I was far too hesitant going into the first corner and braked about five metres too early. That cost me a crucial five places.

And I certainly wasn't forceful enough in the opening two laps to get back right away among the guys who had gone by. When you see raindrops on your visor you are never sure how hard you can push and what you can get away with.

Looking back after the race I am sure that if I had gone balls-out and pushed a good deal harder from the start I could well have been in the frame for fourth place at the end. I was frustrated. But maybe I was being too hard on myself. After all, I moved into fifth place in the championship overall. And after only three races.

I felt that nice and early I had established myself as a threat to the regular front runners, despite being on a steep learning curve in totally different company from my WSB days. I have honestly been amazed how genuinely surprised some people have been at how well I've done, as if I'd never raced at these sorts of levels. I am sure there are people who wanted me to fail for whatever reason, and it is extremely satisfying to prove them wrong.

Up front, well out of my sight, there was a terrific show being staged by my fellow MotoGP rookie Jorge Lorenzo.

He was on unbeatable form and, remarkably, managed to clinch a win, well clear of regular first-across-the-line Valentino Rossi, in only his third race at this level.

*I am sure there are
people who wanted me to fail
for whatever reason, and it is
extremely satisfying to prove them wrong*

It was a sharp lesson for all the regular front runners in MotoGP that a 20-year-old like Jorge could show them all the way home. And it was encouraging for me, too, even though I wasn't directly involved.

Actually, Jorge forced Valentino, his Yamaha teammate, into the longest winless streak of his MotoGP career – seven races without finishing up on the top step of the podium was a wake-up call for him. Knowing the Italian, even as slightly as I do, I would guess that unwanted record will stir him up to a fight-back that will be a reminder to us all of just how great a rider and fearsome competitor he can be.

He led for the opening twelve laps in very tricky and wet conditions as the drizzle dampened the track, and he admitted afterwards that once Jorge had passed him he did not stand a chance of breaking his losing sequence.

Once Jorge had muscled past Rossi and his Spanish rival and not-so-best-friend Pedrosa – a double-whammy on lap thirteen – there was no looking back for him. And, Roger Burnett, who had watched it all on TV in the Yamaha garage, told me later he never seemed to be in any danger.

The victory ranked him the fifth youngest winner in the history of MotoGP.

Valentino was in third place, more than twelve seconds behind at the flag as Jorge vanished over the horizon for his first-ever MotoGP victory.

The result dumped the former champion fourteen points behind joint series leaders Jorge and Dani Pedrosa – but he refused to be downcast, a lesson for us all that there can be a way back if you fight hard enough for it.

I reminded myself that I am the rookie and I must not expect too much too soon

My guess is that it is just what he will do in the upcoming rounds. From what I have seen over the course of his stunning performances, Valentino is at his formidable best when his back is to the wall and the other guys imagine they've got him where they want him. He had ditched his Michelin tyres – the ones I'm happy to race on – for Bridgestones and the decision looked a dubious one as he struggled for rear-end grip on his new and preferred rubber.

He admitted, knowing the track was cruel on Bridgestones, that if he had been offered third place before the race he would have gladly accepted straightaway.

Rossi's long-term crew chief Jerry Burgess was chuffed at Lorenzo's emphatic win and said: 'It was an impressive ride, fantastic, and he really dished it out to everyone – but I thought he could have won in Jerez.'

When it was all totted up Jorge had clinched three pole positions, three podium places, one of them a really great win, in his first three races in the premier class. Amazing. He said: 'I think I'm hallucinating. This is just fantastic.'

I suppose, being pleased at my own start, I could take even more encouragement from Jorge's record: if he can do it, why can't I when I get to grips with the new engine and above five-miles-an-hour more down the straights?

It was, I felt, ironic that just when the other guys were pinpointing me as being too aggressive, it was a lack of aggression that cost me dearly in this race

OK, a lot of the tracks, like here in Estoril, and the next one in Shanghai, are new to me and that, of course, can be something of a disadvantage. But I'm a quick learner and I'm not going to sit behind that sort of excuse for not improving on my encouraging start.

It is in my nature to fight back against the odds, as I have done all my life, and that is just what I shall be endeavouring to do when we get to China and I get a little more familiar with the new motor.

Roger is insisting I be patient and his advice, offered before and after every race, is a valuable key to my progress. He doesn't let me get away with anything that he feels is not right for my career, on track or off. And it is a friendship, and a wise and honest, if forthright, counsel, I appreciate.

The more I am around the Tech 3 set-up, and Yamaha, the more I am convinced I made the right move. They have promised me full factory support with a 2009 YZR-M1 to test right from the start of the long pre-season effort. What could be better?

A factory bike for 2009, the absolute and total backing of Yamaha and a great team that has made me right at home, a very experienced boss in Herve, and all of the best that can be offered, just as it has been with Valentino Rossi. Money can't buy any of that.

It is in my nature to fight back against the odds, as I have done all my life

Pos	Pts	No	Rider	Nation	Team	Bike	Total time
1	25	48	Jorge Lorenzo	SPA	Fiat Yamaha Team	Yamaha	45'53.098
2	20	2	Dani Pedrosa	SPA	Repsol Honda Team	Honda	45'54.906
3	16	46	Valentino Rossi	ITA	Fiat Yamaha Team	Yamaha	46'05.812
4	13	5	Colin Edwards	USA	Tech 3 Yamaha	Yamaha	46'10.312
5	11	21	John Hopkins	USA	Kawasaki Racing Team	Kawasaki	46'16.814
6	10	1	Casey Stoner	AUS	Ducati Marlboro Team	Ducati	46'19.777
7	9	52	James Toseland	GBR	Tech 3 Yamaha	Yamaha	46'25.720
8	8	7	Chris Vermeulen	AUS	Rizla Suzuki MotoGP	Suzuki	46'29.471
9	7	64	Loris Capirossi	ITA	Rizla Suzuki MotoGP	Suzuki	46'31.357
10	6	56	Shinya Nakano	JPN	San Carlo Honda Gresini	Honda	46'32.565
11	5	15	Alex de Angelis	RSM	San Carlo Honda Gresini	Honda	46'54.395
12	4	24	Toni Elias	SPA	Alice Team	Ducati	46'56.956
13	3	33	Marco Melandri	ITA	Ducati Marlboro Team	Ducati	47'02.614
14	2	50	Sylvain Guintoli	FRA	Alice Team	Ducati	47'02.723
15	1	14	Randy de Puniet	FRA	LCR Honda MotoGP	Honda	47'04.631
16		13	Anthony West	AUS	Kawasaki Racing Team	Kawasaki	47'16.718
			Not classified				
		69	Nicky Hayden	USA	Repsol Honda Team	Honda	26'23.675
		4	Andrea Dovizioso	ITA	JiR Team Scot MotoGP	Honda	24'43.870

▶ Left to right: Ducati team boss Livio Suppo, Dani Pedrosa, Valentino Rossi and Loris Capirossi.

*I am sold on MotoGP —
and I want to rise to the
top of the pile*

And it is my affirmed intention to give back as much effort as they are prepared to put into me. I am sold on MotoGP – and I want to rise to the top of the pile.

But, as anybody who knows me would agree, I never take anything for granted. I don't expect to be given anything I haven't worked for. I have been out of work and I have known the misery of not having a ride, which was the case for me through the winter of 2005. It taught me a lesson – that even though you are number one in the world, as I was with the WSB title, you can lose it all.

My dream now, and it is slowly taking shape, is to give it my best shot, 110 per cent all the time, to win the MotoGP crown and, at the same, the respect of my peers in this very tough and unforgiving sport.

CHINA

Shanghai Circuit, 4 May

I suppose I should have been thankful for small mercies and contented myself with the knowledge that I did at least finish the race . . .

I will be doing my best to make up for any lack of circuit familiarity with my usual determination and spirit

After such an encouraging start to my MotoGP career I realised that, sooner or later, it was going to be come-uppance time when I got to circuits like Shanghai, which was completely new territory to me.

That realisation did not, of course, hold me back in any way from giving it my all, despite my crucial lack of familiarity with the Chinese track. But, try as I might, I could make no impression on the outcome of the race to add to my opening run of three successive top seven finishes.

China is a long way to travel for a race. But it seems like ten times the distance when you are coming home after a massive disappointment like the one I had in Shanghai. On the plane home my mind could only focus on what went wrong.

But the long flight back gave me plenty of time to think over my deep upset and work out that my MotoGP learning curve was getting steeper and that, as a consequence, I would have to learn to be more patient.

My lack of knowhow around Shanghai, along with one hell of a struggle to find the right set-up, conspired to leave me struggling against guys much deeper down the field than I had been used to battling against, and I just sank progressively lower and lower until I motored home in twelfth place from seventh on the grid.

*No matter how hard
I rode — and I certainly
did get stuck in — I
was going nowhere fast*

I just could not defend myself against the likes of Marco Melandri, Shinya Nakano, Toni Elias and Loris Capirossi, all riders who seemed rejuvenated in China and who showed me that I still have a good way to go and a lot to learn. One by one all these guys buzzed by me and dropped me off – and the front tyre I had on was not helping either.

It is terribly disappointing, not to mention deflating, to be overtaken by all these guys and not be able to retaliate and fight back as is my nature. But no matter how hard I rode – and I certainly did get stuck in – I was going nowhere fast.

When I was on the brakes the transfer of weight was really quick so whenever I turned in the rear wheel was skating all over the shop. It was not planted on the way into the corners. I had to wait far too long for it to load up again before I dared get on the power.

That's the problem with 800s – they lack the necessary torque and you just have to keep up the corner speed constant to try and benefit. If you are struggling to get into the corner and carry the speed through you can't square anything off, so I was finding it difficult on both the entry and the exit. That made me slow mid-corner, and getting out and losing time like that can cost you as much as one second a lap. It might not sound like much, but I can tell you it's a massive mountain of time to make up in a race against guys as good and as quick as these in MotoGP.

What with not knowing the track, despite the best efforts of the guys in the garage to help me out, and my having a rotten set-up my chances were swiftly diminished and my race compromised.

Up front the race developed into a two-horse chase with Pedrosa and Rossi really snapping hard at each other in a spectacular tussle that had the crowd really tuned in. It was down to them for the main show as the rest of us trailed in their wake a considerable distance behind.

Then Valentino, as can be his wont when he's in the mood, cleared off at record-shattering pace and broke a seven-race losing streak with a great win, the fourth different rider to triumph in four races so far.

I saw none of this, of course, locked as I was, initially, down among the midfielders then, as the race ebbed away, floundering with the also-rans. I got off to a decent start, but found it really difficult with the setting I had. We gambled with it for the race, and on paper it looked OK, but unfortunately it was not quite right and it cost me loads of time in crucial places. That was the difference between being, say, in the top eight or down in twelfth place.

My teammate Colin Edwards grabbed the third pole of his MotoGP career, and Tech 3 Yamaha's first, with the fastest-ever lap of Shanghai, but he fell away in the race after overshooting and running off the track at the end of the back straight on lap six. Rossi and Pedrosa had cleared off by then, but he had been holding onto third place, pulling nicely ahead of Casey Stoner, when he overdid it and lost four places. Try as hard as he did he just couldn't regain the lost ground. And he finished eighth with enough points to claim seventh place in the championship and drop in just behind me, on 33 points, equal with Capirossi.

I just could not defend myself against the likes of Melandri, Nakano, Elias and Capirossi

▲ Jorge Lorenzo's spectacular crash during testing.

The amazing cameo of the race was Jorge Lorenzo's gutsy performance. He'd had the most horrendously spectacular crash, somersaulting about ten feet over the high side and smashing his ankle, on Friday morning.

He reckoned afterwards that the crash was due to the fact that he had not let his Michelin rear tyre get up to a working temperature, but his crew chief, Ramon

Forcada, argued it was caused by a small wheelie as he gassed it, pushing hard and switching direction, 250cc-style, out of turn one towards the next downhill left-hander.

Jorge admitted afterwards it was the biggest crash of his career. It was certainly scary to see – but it didn't put him off and in the race, two days later, he was in cracking form whatever pain and discomfort he was suffering due to his broken bones and battered body.

We've all done it. We've all come back as soon as we could after enormous accidents that would put normal folk off riding bikes for life. It's our livelihood and you cannot afford to be scared off by crashes that are part and parcel of this job. The trick is to get right back on the bike as soon as possible. No point in being scared.

► Valentino celebrates his first win of the season.

I suppose I should have been thankful for small mercies and contented myself with the knowledge that I did at least finish the race – yet again, despite my troubles – albeit not where I wanted to be placed, but I was still running at the close and prepared to pick up any crumbs.

Pos	Pts	No	Rider	Nation	Team	Bike	Total time
1	25	46	Valentino Rossi	ITA	Fiat Yamaha Team	Yamaha	44'08.061
2	20	2	Dani Pedrosa	SPA	Repsol Honda Team	Honda	44'11.951
3	16	1	Casey Stoner	AUS	Ducati Marlboro Team	Ducati	44'23.989
4	13	48	Jorge Lorenzo	SPA	Fiat Yamaha Team	Yamaha	44'30.555
5	11	33	Marco Melandri	ITA	Ducati Marlboro Team	Ducati	44'35.018
6	10	69	Nicky Hayden	USA	Repsol Honda Team	Honda	44'36.430
7	9	5	Colin Edwards	USA	Tech 3 Yamaha	Yamaha	44'37.841
8	8	24	Toni Elias	SPA	Alice Team	Ducati	44'38.286
9	7	64	Loris Capirossi	ITA	Rizla Suzuki MotoGP	Suzuki	44'39.501
10	6	56	Shinya Nakano	JPN	San Carlo Honda Gresini	Honda	44'44.030
11	5	4	Andrea Dovizioso	ITA	JiR Team Scot MotoGP	Honda	44'44.307
12	4	52	James Toseland	GBR	Tech 3 Yamaha	Yamaha	44'51.252
13	3	14	Randy de Puniet	FRA	LCR Honda MotoGP	Honda	44'51.503
14	2	21	John Hopkins	USA	Kawasaki Racing Team	Kawasaki	44'53.916
15	1	50	Sylvain Guintoli	FRA	Alice Team	Ducati	44'54.391
16		15	Alex de Angelis	RSM	San Carlo Honda Gresini	Honda	44'58.654
17		13	Anthony West	AUS	Kawasaki Racing Team	Kawasaki	45'13.654
			Not classified				
		7	Chris Vermeulen	AUS	Rizla Suzuki MotoGP	Suzuki	12'37.734

CHINA ROUND 4

RESULTS

Twelfth, I reminded myself, was not where I plan to be. But in my first season this level of result is going to happen.

To say I was happy to put Shanghai behind me is an understatement, but it alerted me to the fact that track knowledge is vital if you want to be on the pace. And with Le Mans coming up I'll have the same problem, but I will be doing my best to make up for any lack of circuit familiarity with my usual determination and spirit.

Just to get myself closer and more deeply involved in the Tech 3 family atmosphere, I have bought a house not far from the factory in Bormes les Mimosas in the south of France and, in between a few promotional dates in Poland and the UK and the Le Mans race, I'll be furnishing the place for nice long summertime stopovers.

To say I was happy to put Shanghai behind me is an understatement

FRANCE

Le Mans, 18 May

'Toseland needs to calm down a bit. He was a little too aggressive where there was no room to pass'

ANDREA DOVIZIOSO

L e Mans, round five, was a personal disaster and the sooner I forget this French farce the better.

It was yet another case of me facing a big setback because I didn't know the track and its vagaries, and I had to cope with a rush of heavily committed riders on unfamiliar territory while still striving to maintain the momentum I had built up in the earlier rounds.

We all realised and appreciated – me, the team and Roger – that a clear problem would be my lack of circuit knowledge at certain venues. Le Mans was one of them.

I'm not making excuses, but when you have to take on the world's quickest and finest riders and give it your all without the essential help of knowing where you are going, it is a major hurdle to overcome. Dangerous, too.

A clear problem would be my lack of circuit knowledge at certain venues. Le Mans was one of them

I struggled through the second free practice session after logging tenth quickest on my first look at the Bugatti circuit in the morning. I was pretty pleased with myself. The afternoon, however, was a different matter altogether and I dropped back to fifteenth. The problem was, we made some changes in the hope of making an improvement on the morning time, but we ended up going backwards. We altered the suspension in an effort to improve the tyre grip and it turned out to be the wrong move. It was more of an annoyance than a really big problem and I knew the boys in the garage would sort it out.

As it turned out, they managed to get things reasonably together for Saturday afternoon and I qualified in a respectable seventh, a place behind ex-champion Nicky Hayden, with Dani Pedrosa on pole from my teammate Colin Edwards. Casey Stoner was third fastest, Valentino Rossi fourth and the amazing patched-up and pieced-together Jorge Lorenzo fifth. I couldn't believe it – the first nine qualifiers were separated by less than one second!

I couldn't believe it — the first nine qualifiers were separated by less than one second!

I never quite managed to get all the corners flowing smoothly together

I was disappointed I just missed out on a second-row placing but I never quite managed to get all the corners flowing smoothly together. I just wished we could start practice at these new circuits on a Tuesday or a Wednesday!

In the race I got off to an encouraging start, a real flyer, and made it into fifth place by the end of the first of the twenty-eight-lap chase. And that gave me a tremendous boost to my confidence – but it was a short-lived high.

John Hopkins, who had started two places behind me, pulled a heavy move on me and nearly put me off the track. It cost me, but I would have done the same to him under the circumstances and I am not going to moan about it, unlike some I know.

I had already had a ding-dong with Andrea Dovizioso when we had swapped places a couple of times, and I was aiming to make up for lost ground when we dipped into lap three. By then I was getting a bit frustrated because I'd had such a great start, but now here I was, ninth, and stuck behind Chris Vermeulen.

He was my next target, but Andrea came by me and, right away, I tried to overtake him to regain the position I'd just lost to him. He made a slight mistake and ran wide. I took that error of his as an opportunity and dived underneath him. But he came back on the line and took my front wheel. Down I went and out of the race, luckily without a scratch. The collision dropped him to fourteenth place and he faced a tough fight-back.

My feeling was that it was just a racing incident, typical of those you see a hundred times when the action is as closely fought as it is at the top level. I doubt he even saw me, but those opening couple of laps were absolute mayhem with plenty of close-up tussling and no quarter given or asked. It is in free-for-alls like that where you need not only the speed and the balls to go for it, but also the track knowledge to carry you through without worrying what corner or problem is looming.

Those opening couple of laps were absolute mayhem with plenty of close-up tussling and no quarter given or asked

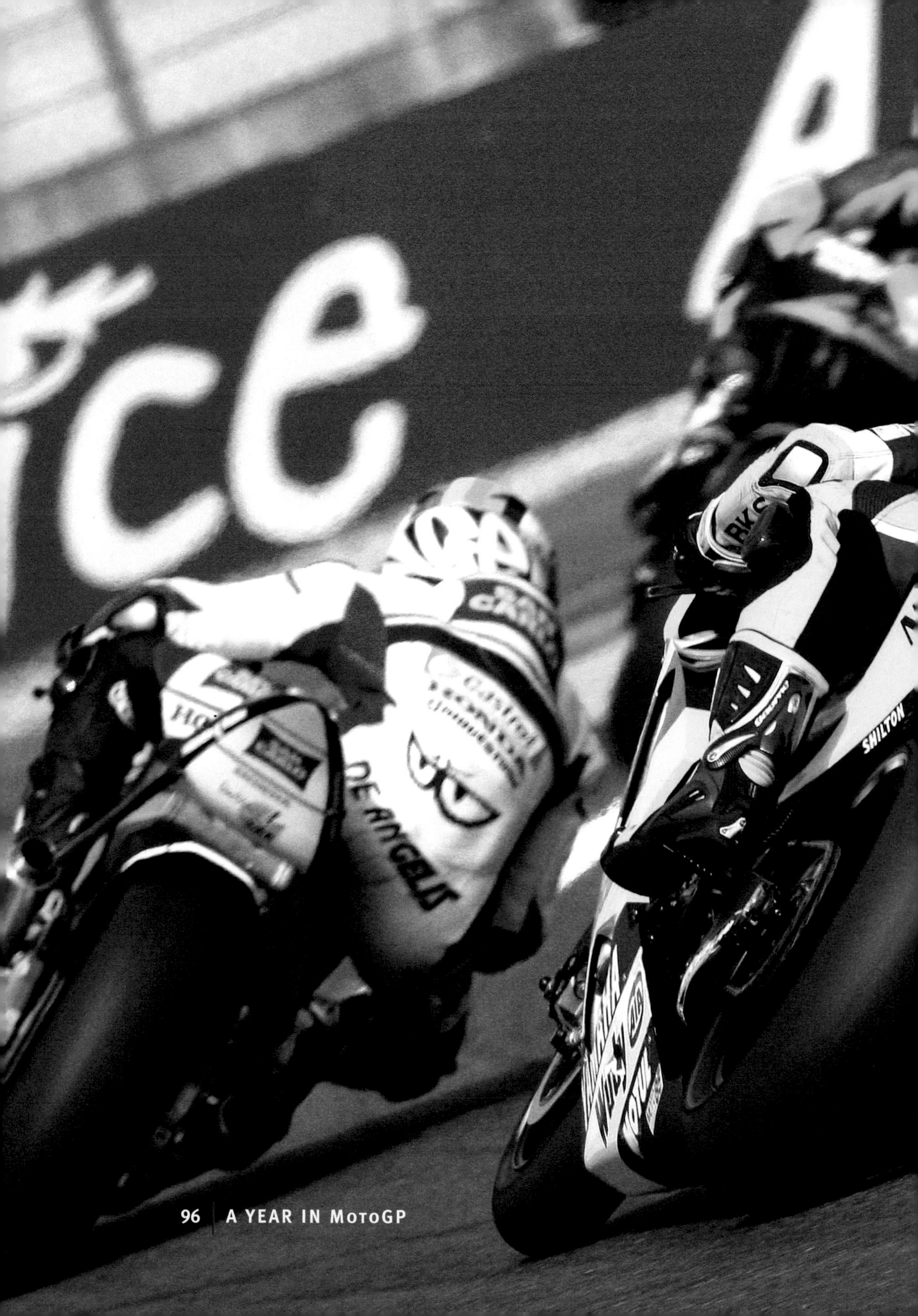
SHILTON

I was certainly the innocent victim and came off worse, not that Dovizioso, with whom I'd already had a few paint-swapping moments in previous races, saw it that way. He reckoned I was to blame and cost him the chance of his first-ever podium in the top ranks. As it was he did well and recovered to finish sixth.

He did say afterwards, 'I am upset because I believe I could have had a podium place.

'I was in front of Jorge Lorenzo when this crash happened – and he went on to finish in second place.

'OK, I'm not claiming I could have run at his pace but I did finish sixth and it is obvious that the incident with James cost me a lot of time.'

Then came the words I totally disagree with, an echo of some of the other guys I had tangled with over the previous races. He went on, 'Toseland needs to calm down a bit. He was a little too aggressive where there was no room to pass.' Join the club, Andrea . . .

It was a big disappointment for me because I, and the team, had been really pleased with my progress when I had claimed top-six finishes in the first two events to boost me into an amazing joint fifth place in the championship. I dropped down to ninth place with my first non-finish, but even though I was bitterly disappointed and frustrated at falling off, I promised the lads back in the garage that I would bounce back and rediscover the momentum I had built up so effectively from the start of the season.

Valentino celebrating another win with Spanish legend Angel Nieto.

It was a memorable day for Rossi. He equalled Spanish legend Angel Nieto's record of ninety Grand Prix wins – and the old champ celebrated and saluted Valentino's achievement by riding pillion to him on the Fiat Yamaha.

Lorenzo, still suffering from two broken ankles from his China spill, and despite crashing twice in practice in Le Mans, was second and Colin Edwards third – and that gave Yamaha their first podium take-over in the premier class for seven years.

I was bitterly disappointed and frustrated at falling off

Pos	Pts	No	Rider	Nation	Team	Bike	Total time
1	25	46	Valentino Rossi	ITA	Fiat Yamaha Team	Yamaha	44'30.799
2	20	48	Jorge Lorenzo	SPA	Fiat Yamaha Team	Yamaha	44'35.796
3	16	5	Colin Edwards	USA	Tech 3 Yamaha	Yamaha	44'37.604
4	13	2	Dani Pedrosa	SPA	Repsol Honda Team	Honda	44'40.956
5	11	7	Chris Vermeulen	AUS	Rizla Suzuki MotoG	Suzuki	44'52.561
6	10	4	Andrea Dovizioso	ITA	JiR Team Scot MotoGP	Honda	44'53.194
7	9	64	Loris Capirossi	ITA	Rizla Suzuki MotoGP	Suzuki	44'58.605
8	8	69	Nicky Hayden	USA	Repsol Honda Team	Honda	44'58.794
9	7	14	Randy de Puniet	FRA	LCR Honda MotoGP	Honda	45'00.143
10	6	56	Shinya Nakano	JPN	San Carlo Honda Gresini	Honda	45'01.621
11	5	24	Toni Elias	SPA	Alice Team	Ducati	45'05.953
12	4	15	Alex de Angelis	RSM	San Carlo Honda Gresini	Honda	45'07.015
13	3	50	Sylvain Guintoli	FRA	Alice Team	Ducati	45'22.837
14	2	13	Anthony West	AUS	Kawasaki Racing Team	Kawasaki	46'00.106
15	1	33	Marco Melandri	ITA	Ducati Marlboro Team	Ducati	46'10.422
16		1	Casey Stoner	AUS	Ducati Marlboro Team	Ducati	44'47.085
			Not classified				
		21	John Hopkins	USA	Kawasaki Racing Team	Kawasaki	25'36.029
		52	**James Toseland**	**GBR**	**Tech 3 Yamaha**	**Yamaha**	**3'19.828**

FRANCE ROUND 5

RESULTS

ITALY

Mugello, 1 June

Being back in the top half-dozen was a massive lift

Round six was taking place on the track where Valentino Rossi had not lost in seven outings. Follow that!

My feeling in the run-up to the race at Mugello, another of the eleven tracks that is new to me, was definitely, Here we go again! Although, I have to confess, I did have a run-out around the place in 2004 thanks to Ducati, who gave me a day out on a MotoGP bike as a present for winning the World Superbike championship. So I had at least a vague idea which way the track went. How much help that would be was something I wondered about in the build-up to the Italian Grand Prix.

It was clear to me that I had been at a severe disadvantage in the last three races on unfamiliar territory and, frustratingly, I had felt one step behind everybody else. So it was a relief to have an outing on a circuit I had at least seen before, despite a few newspaper reports to the contrary.

My concerns to get my show back on the road and do well after that disappointing twelfth in Shanghai and a disastrous crash in Le Mans were my driving force for round six, which was taking place on the track where Valentino Rossi had not lost in seven outings. Follow that!

I got off to a flyer in absolutely appalling rainy conditions for free practice. In fact, in the second session, in a blinding downpour, I fronted the action from well before the halfway stage by as much as 2.585 seconds. And it all lasted until the last few minutes when conditions improved and the other guys made up ground on my time and I dropped down to fifth quickest. But I was still only a very satisfying 0.085 seconds behind Valentino, the Mugello specialist who was hitting top form again.

I have to pay tribute to my teammate Colin Edwards, as nice a guy as there is and as good and helpful a partner as you could have in a team, for helping me overcome the problem that was hindering my progress: my settings. We talked over the issue and his suggestions vastly improved the bike's performance and my confidence in it.

I came away from Mugello a much more contented guy with a good set-up which, hopefully, will boost me back to where I started the season with regular high placings. It certainly showed its value in Italy.

I ran the shorter wheelbase that other Yamaha riders had been using and it gave me much more confidence in the rear end, especially in the wet

Basically, I ran the shorter wheelbase that other Yamaha riders had been using and it gave me much more confidence in the rear end, especially in the wet. Before Saturday's qualifying and after the morning warm-up we made the alterations. They amounted to taking a link out of the chain which moved the rear wheel about 12–16mm forward. That made the bike shorter – but a bit more nervous, too.

The front end flapped about so dramatically between the corners that the lads in the garage pulled in my handlebars to compensate – and it all worked brilliantly. The extra weight forced onto the back end made all the difference. There was a bigger contact patch which filled me with plenty of confidence to push really hard. I think Colin was as pleased as I was at the outcome of his suggestion. I was certainly grateful and I reckoned myself lucky to have a teammate who didn't just think selfishly about his own performance all the time.

Sure, it was all a gamble. But, really, I had nothing to lose. I was anxious to get back to the level of performance I had shown in Qatar and Spain when I had hit sixth place each time.

It is in the record books now, but that is just what I managed to do, and on a track I was still learning as I went. My 'slump', my lowly place in China and my crash in France, as it had been described in the specialist press, was now written off as a 'minor blip'.

It took a lot of effort all the same. I had qualified eighth, but lost three places on lap one after some near paint swapping with Shinya Nakano. But I managed to keep calm and not go looking for instant retribution.

Instead I bided my time and did not do anything wild or stupid. I made up two places on the second lap with a bit of hard, but safe, riding and another into ninth place on lap three. Rossi had by then gone ahead, looking for his third win in a row, his 91st career victory. He, of course, was way out of my sight.

I put a move on Colin Edwards and passed him from ninth to seventh place, and then found myself locked in a scrap with Alex de Angelis, on the Gresini Honda, until he cleared off to finish fourth – a great result for a lad who had more of a reputation as a crasher.

I put a move on Colin Edwards and passed him from ninth to seventh place, and then found myself locked in a scrap with Alex de Angelis

Jorge Lorenzo, riding with broken ankles, fell off after six laps and that promoted me a place, but left me tangling with Shinya Nakano and Nicky Hayden and Italian heroes Andrea Dovizioso – the cause of my Le Mans downfall – and Loris Capirossi.

It was all thrilling stuff and once I'd overtaken Dovizioso on the inside with thirteen laps to go I was in sixth place. Capirossi was next, done late on the brakes – very late – a lap later and I was up to fifth and feeling extremely confident. Not that Loris was going to let me have it easy. Nor was my pal Colin Edwards at speeds just topping 202mph.

I should have known that Colin would not sit back to enjoy the frantic action in front of him – he's too competitive a guy to do that – and he out-witted me to snatch my fifth place with nine to go. I reasoned then there was no point in risking falling off by doing something silly and trying too hard to regain my fifth spot. I settled for sixth, chased hard right to the flag by Loris.

It was a big relief to finish as high as that because, on Saturday morning, when things were going pretty miserably with the bike and the weather was a real mix of wet and dry, I was getting het up striving to get a suitable and effective setting. As it happened – thanks to Colin and the mechanics – we turned what had threatened to be a lousy chance into a top-six finisher.

And being back in the top half-dozen, with a heap of fast guys either crashed or behind me, was a massive lift. I admit I had not been too happy with the results leading up to Mugello because I had set myself some pretty high standards.

I would love to have gone one better and finished fifth as a just reward for all the effort I put into what was a really tough, but thoroughly enjoyable, race. Looking back I have to be happy – I am in eighth place in the championship, three points clear of ex-champion Nicky Hayden, and, after Barcelona, with some tracks I am familiar with coming up.

I tell myself not to allow my morale to be dented while I am still on a learning curve as a MotoGP rookie. And having been WSB champion twice counts for nothing now. If I was riding as hard as I am right now and finishing down the field among the also-rans my confidence would be really damaged. But I feel I am riding well and competitively, trying to give nothing away or yielding any ground that the others don't have to work hard to steal from me.

What's more, I'm gelling with the team and we are getting the package right for the upcoming action.

If I do have a self-criticism it is this: I have plenty of room yet for further improvement in my riding style. Not my aggression or ability to overtake, I am happy with that. My throttle control needs a bit of work on it. I am a bit too heavy on it between the corners and that prevents me from flowing as freely and as easily as I would like and as, I know, would benefit me. The problem is that I am just too eager to get the bike to its flat-out pace and I need more restraint to urge more corner speed out of it.

Pos	Pts	No	Rider	Nation	Team	Bike	Total time
1	25	46	Valentino Rossi	ITA	Fiat Yamaha Team	Yamaha	42'31.153
2	20	1	Casey Stoner	AUS	Ducati Marlboro Team	Ducati	42'33.354
3	16	2	Dani Pedrosa	SPA	Repsol Honda Team	Honda	42'36.020
4	13	15	Alex de Angelis	RSM	San Carlo Honda Gresini	Honda	42'37.466
5	11	5	Colin Edwards	USA	Tech 3 Yamaha	Yamaha	42'43.683
6	10	52	James Toseland	GBR	Tech 3 Yamaha	Yamaha	42'44.959
7	9	64	Loris Capirossi	ITA	Rizla Suzuki MotoGP	Suzuki	42'44.959
8	8	4	Andrea Dovizioso	ITA	JiR Team Scot MotoGP	Honda	42'46.472
9	7	56	Shinya Nakano	JPN	San Carlo Honda Gresini	Honda	42'46.480
10	6	7	Chris Vermeulen	AUS	Rizla Suzuki MotoGP	Suzuki	43'01.938
11	5	50	Sylvain Guintoli	FRA	Alice Team	Ducati	43'10.744
12	4	24	Toni Elias	SPA	Alice Team	Ducati	43'21.174
13	3	69	Nicky Hayden	USA	Repsol Honda Team	Honda	43'21.593
14	2	8	Tadayuki Okada	JPN	Repsol Honda Team	Honda	43'30.002
15	1	13	Anthony West	AUS	Kawasaki Racing Team	Kawasaki	43'31.889
			Not classified				
		48	Jorge Lorenzo	SPA	Fiat Yamaha Team	Yamaha	11'11.489
		21	John Hopkins	USA	Kawasaki Racing Team	Kawasaki	11'17.629
		14	Randy de Puniet	FRA	LCR Honda MotoGP	Honda	9'25.989
		33	Marco Melandri	ITA	Ducati Marlboro Team	Ducati	9'26.358

**ITALY
ROUND 6**

RESULTS

Looking back I have to be happy — I am in eighth place in the championship, three points clear of ex-champion Nicky Hayden

CATALUNYA

Circuit de Catalunya, 8 June

'James is doing a great, great job — now he has to understand how to improve, but for somebody in his debut year, it is not so bad. He will be a big threat at Donington.' VALENTINO ROSSI

I have no complaints – unlike a few other guys I know – when what I dish out in the heat of the split second is returned in handfuls

I came away from the Catalunya Grand Prix feeling a mixture of satisfaction yet disappointment too, when I added up the high and low points from an eventful weekend. On one hand, I felt I had made a breakthrough and shown myself to be a genuine threat to the front runners. But on the other I was desperately disappointed that I had not done better than my sixth place.

It was the first time I came into close contact with Valentino Rossi. In all the previous races he had already cleared off by the time I got settled into the action. But this time around in Barcelona he was behind me on the grid after messing up his qualifying session. And if being hunted down by the legend wasn't enough to give me the urge to give it my best, then I didn't know what would be. The prospect was both daunting and exciting. Me, new to the place and without a clue which way the circuit went, and Valentino, who knew every twist and turn.

It was going to be a real challenge with the double trouble of trying to outwit probably the best bike racer the world has ever seen on yet another track completely unfamiliar to me.

It was clearly a case of, Ah well, let's get on with it. I'll try and pick up as much knowledge as I can as I go. I covered a few laps running – that way you get the idea of the lay of the place. But there's a big difference between hitting a corner at 4mph on foot and 150mph on tyres that want to slide and pitch you off.

Poor old Jorge Lorenzo, a crash waiting to happen at every race, was off yet again at 80mph on lap five of Friday's free practice session. He was so badly concussed he couldn't tell the doctors what class he was racing in. This time it was serious enough for him to be kept in hospital for 48 hours and, of course, he missed the race on Sunday.

Casey Stoner topped the time sheets. I was sixth fastest just behind my Tech 3 Yamaha teammate Colin Edwards. So I was all set for a real ding-dong with him to chase and Valentino to keep at bay.

If all those critics who have slammed me for being aggressive had been aboard with me when Rossi came by they would have realised that, right down the line in MotoGP, from top to bottom, there is a necessary level of determination and commitment that crucially transcends any surrender when you are striving to hang onto what you have earned.

I have no complaints – unlike a few other guys I know – when what I dish out in the heat of the split second is returned in handfuls. And Valentino's pass on me into the first corner on lap two was uncompromising and tough.

He forced me to run off onto the tarmac in a real braking showdown but, hey, that's all part and parcel of the tactics. Ask nothing, give nothing, take what you can, when you can . . . or don't call yourself a racer.

Valentino is a switched-on competitor, very clever, fearless and ruthless too, and he makes sure you feel the impact of his bravery

I managed another sixth place for the fourth time in seven races — and only Valentino overtook more riders than I did

Valentino is a switched-on competitor, very clever, fearless and ruthless too, and he makes sure you feel the impact of his bravery, his daring and his downright ability and experience if you are in his way.

He came up from behind me and just kept his bike alongside mine, deeper and deeper, so I could not turn in. If I had been overly bold and tried to tip the bike into the corner I would not only have risked a pile-up trying to keep the brake on into the turn to make it through safely, but I'd have gone into turn two so deep I'd have lost valuable places.

The best option for me was to go straight over the tarmac and get back into the race that way. There was no way I was ready to let him pass, but he just let off his brakes at the same time as me to keep in my way.

We were both letting off the stoppers and by the time we were set to turn in we were going too fast – he had to let off and run out wide. Unfortunately for me I was on the outside of him and so bloody close, but luckily there was no contact between us. I was not going to be intimidated, stubborn guy that I am. But by the time we had hit the turn-in point we were both going far too fast, he was too deep, and that's how I got pushed wide by him.

It was all pretty dodgy and hectic, but it was a clean move on his part – nothing wrong with it, no complaints from me. And If I'd been in his boots I'd have done exactly the same. I probably have done already.

I had one hell of a scrap from then on in and passed Nicky Hayden, Alex de Angelis, Chris Vermeulen and Loris Capirossi in a very enjoyable and exciting charge through the field, from down to eleventh at one stage.

Valentino, who rode brilliantly, went on to finish second, but he couldn't close down Dani Pedrosa, who had a runaway win. Casey Stoner was third.

The first four or five laps
are so important and if you lose out so
early it is one hell of a job to win back the lost ground

I managed another sixth place for the fourth time in seven races – and only Valentino overtook more riders than I did. Even so, I was really disappointed that I had not done better, say a fourth place.

When I first started scoring sixth places I felt that was as good as it could get because I felt I could not go any better. But now I am getting frustrated because I am sure I can do much better. I feel a mixture of contentment because of how well people, and my team, tell me I am doing, and frustration because I firmly and honestly believe I am worth higher placings. The bike feels good now and the boys in the garage and Herve, my boss, are a fantastic boost to my confidence.

I have to admit that my starts, those essential get-aways with the guys on the opening few laps, could be better and more effective. I've learned that the first four or five laps are so important and if you lose out so early it is one hell of a job to win back the lost ground.

That is an aspect of my racing that I shall be working on for Donington Park when I go looking for my first podium. And I will at last be on a track I know well, with, I believe, the support of a massive crowd. It can't come soon enough for me.

I just hope I can live up to Valentino's praises: 'James is doing a great, great job – now he has to understand how to improve, but for somebody in his debut year, it is not so bad. He will be a big threat at Donington.'

The bike feels good now and the boys in the garage and Herve, my boss, are a fantastic boost to my confidence

Pos	Pts	No	Rider	Nation	Team	Bike	Total time
1	25	2	Dani Pedrosa	SPA	Repsol Honda Team	Honda	43'02.175
2	20	46	Valentino Rossi	ITA	Fiat Yamaha Team	Yamaha	43'04.981
3	16	1	Casey Stoner	AUS	Ducati Marlboro Team	Ducati	43'05.518
4	13	4	Andrea Dovizioso	ITA	JiR Team Scot MotoGP	Honda	43'13.068
5	11	5	Colin Edwards	USA	Tech 3 Yamaha	Yamaha	43'18.601
6	10	52	James Toseland	GBR	Tech 3 Yamaha	Yamaha	43'23.657
7	9	7	Chris Vermeulen	AUS	Rizla Suzuki MotoGP	Suzuki	43'23.723
8	8	69	Nicky Hayden	USA	Repsol Honda Team	Honda	43'24.455
9	7	56	Shinya Nakano	JPN	San Carlo Honda Gresini	Honda	43'24.550
10	6	21	John Hopkins	USA	Kawasaki Racing Team	Kawasaki	43'49.010
11	5	33	Marco Melandri	ITA	Ducati Marlboro Team	Ducati	44'00.166
12	4	13	Anthony West	AUS	Kawasaki Racing Team	Kawasaki	44'01.343
13	3	50	Sylvain Guintoli	FRA	Alice Team	Ducati	44'02.954
			Not classified				
		14	Randy de Puniet	FRA	LCR Honda MotoGP	Honda	19'01.576
		15	Alex de Angelis	RSM	San Carlo Honda Gresini	Honda	17'23.460
		64	Loris Capirossi	ITA	Rizla Suzuki MotoGP	Suzuki	17'23.501
			Excluded				
		24	Toni Elias	SPA	Alice Team	Ducati	

CATALUNYA
ROUND 7

RESULTS

GREAT BRITAIN

Donington Park, 22 June

I could not do anything other than go out there and do my best for all those fans. That is why I was pushing so hard and got myself in trouble.

More than 88,000 spectators turned up, I guessed mainly in the hope of seeing me put in a performance strong enough to at least get onto the podium said I wanted to give my fans something to remember. And I did, but for all the wrong reasons.

My British Grand Prix debut at a sell-out Donington Park, the nearest track to my birthplace of Sheffield, was a total disaster, a nightmare, and the worst day of my racing life.

More than 88,000 spectators turned up, I guessed mainly in the hope of seeing me put in a performance strong enough to at least get onto the podium. That was not only my aim; it was also my genuine belief that I could do it, in the light of my steady progress and the gradual increase in my bike's performance and my growing knowledge and confidence in it.

It turned out that there was a great show from a Brit – but it wasn't me. That privilege fell to Scott Redding, an amazing 15-year-old schoolboy who did both the brilliant and the unexpected by clinching victory in the 125cc race, the youngest ever winner of the Grand Prix, and the first UK-born racer to hit the top in this category since Charles Mortimer in Spain in 1973.

In stark contrast to Scott's success and his obvious pride and joy, my entire weekend was one of gloom and heartbreak. I made a hash of the job and I cannot apologise enough to all those supportive people who paid good money in the hope that I would follow through on my pre-race prediction to get at least a top three place.

The whole sorry business on this highly forgettable weekend began on Saturday. I fell off three times whilst striving to qualify in a place high enough to give me a fair chance of mixing it with the regular front runners.

I was off at Coppice in the morning session, unhurt thank goodness, and in the afternoon, when it was most crucial, I was making a late bid to boost my grid position in treacherously wet and slippery conditions. But disaster struck – twice in about half a mile.

I was running twelfth when I high-sided off as I gassed it out of Goddards, the last bend before the start and finish line. I got back on but was down again at Starkey's Bridge, mercifully again unhurt except for badly damaged pride. Talk about embarrassment!

I fell off three times whilst striving to qualify in a place high enough to give me a fair chance of mixing it with the regular front runners

The real setback was that I was shoved onto the sixth row of the grid. Basically I made a mess of it. The potential for a top six was there, but I bungled the job. I tried a few things that didn't work and I felt I was on the edge of the setting.

I changed a few things but we never went in a positive direction. We were fast running out of time and that put me under more pressure to get in a good lap right at the end of qualifying. But I got on the throttle too early at Goddards and high-sided and damaged the rear brake. It engaged the brake itself and chucked me off again inside about half a mile. I failed to make the most of my best qualifying tyre and then I pushed a bit too hard on rubber that was not right for the job.

That said, I could not do anything other than go out there and do my best for all those fans. That is why I was pushing so hard and got myself in trouble.

The marshals at the spot for my third crash were brilliant, true heroes, they tried to get me going again and risked a lot because it was a really busy and dodgy part of the circuit.

I was devastated to finish sixteenth quickest, my worst qualifying position in MotoGP, with two sore knees. In the morning accident the handlebar hit my right knee and in the afternoon the crash in a fast section bashed me about a bit, but not enough to threaten my race. What the falls did was make me more determined to put on a show for the fans, even if I was going to be right up against it being so far back on the grid. I knew I was quicker than eight or so of the guys in front of me.

I was determined to give it my best shot to make up for the dreadful disappointment. I could not have imagined in my wildest dreams that things were going to get even worse.

I had been so looking forward to my MotoGP debut on home soil and had happily involved myself in the pre-race publicity build-up with all sorts of appearances and attendances, including a Donington Park concert with my band Crash before the on-track action got underway.

A criticism that did the rounds was that maybe I had paid too much attention to the peripherals and it had a negative impact on my attitude and concentration, but that's rubbish. Despite all the attention and focus on me, I was really well relaxed without losing sight for one second of the task ahead of me. Being involved with so many activities, like my charity bike ride, away from the hurly-burly of the job, was both a privilege and a great joy, and it raised more than £5,000. And, truth be told, the activities before Saturday and Sunday were a great way for me relax. I didn't understand what the people who criticised me would have preferred me to do – to see nobody and lock myself away in a darkened room right up to the race?

When race day dawned – and better, drier weather with it – I accepted my commitment to it had to be 110 per cent. There was a full house. My mood was one of sheer determination to make up for the failings of the previous day, when qualifying proved to be such a disaster, and I was motivated without being wildly ambitious to at least equal the results I had been consistently recording. But I knew I had my work cut out to make up vital places to establish a good run so I could dial in some consistent laps and get stuck in to some crucial overtaking.

From where I was standing on the grid it seemed miles away from the pole that Casey Stoner had grabbed – some three seconds or so in time and a lifetime in racing terms.

But I was sharpened to the notion that I should go for it. And I did. But I gave it too much. I got off to a cracker of a start and passed I don't know how many guys in the melee before the first turn, Redgate. And that's where it all went sadly wrong.

I was trying too hard. When you start sixteenth you either ride around dumbing it at the back of the pack or go for it. It is my nature to do just that. And I went for it. My feeling was that I was faster than a good half a dozen or more guys ahead of me on the grid and I had every chance of making up some places early on in the race. But I had too much speed into the first corner and the back end stepped out and somersaulted me over the top. End of hope and glory.

There was nobody but me to blame for my crash

This has to be one of the biggest disappointments of my life

'It took a lot of courage for him to carry on when he could easily have come into the garage. But he really wanted to repay the British fans for their support. And that's why he stayed out there'

HERVE PONCHARAL

I hurt my left hand and burned my neck when the tyre hit me as I somersaulted onto the gravel – and, just to make things worse, the right footrest snapped off so I had to balance my foot on the exhaust. In those awful circumstances you do one of two things: quit and motor back to the garage or carry on as best you can and put on some sort of show for the fans and stay out for the thirty laps. The latter is what I opted to do. And it was hell on earth being lapped by guys I know would not have got anywhere near me under regular conditions.

There was nobody but me to blame for my crash – but I would say that the previous day's rotten weather had wrecked my chances of finding a good set-up and I was left with no option but to give it my all without the settings being what they should have been.

Stoner went on to win from Rossi – and I motored home in seventeenth place, head and hand hurting a lot, out of the points, bitterly disappointed and, I confess, with a few tears in my eyes because I had been so fired up to give all the fans something to cheer. I felt I had let them down so badly. To add to my misery I moved down a place to eighth in the championship.

I will bounce back, but this has to be one of the biggest disappointments of my entire career. I know my turn will come if I can keep showing the right attitude and giving it all the effort I can.

Herve, the team boss, was sympathetic and he said afterwards at a press conference: 'I am so disappointed for James, he really wanted to do well. But the rain on Saturday meant he was always up against the clock to improve and get the settings right.

'In the race he made a mistake but I have nothing but huge admiration for what he did afterwards. It look a lot of courage for him to carry on when he could easily have come into the garage. But he really wanted to repay the British fans for their support. And that's why he stayed out there.'

I was at rock bottom. But thanks to a whole wedge of good will messages from the fans on my website, the crowd's encouraging reaction at the end and Herve's and the team's warm words, I felt buoyed up for next week's action in Holland on one of my favourite tracks: Assen.

▶ Donington was a massive disappointment, but I'm determined to come back.

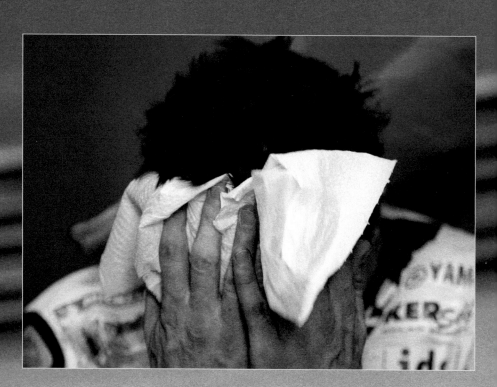

GREAT BRITAIN
ROUND 8

RESULTS

Pos	Pts	No	Rider	Nation	Team	Bike	Total time
1	25	1	Casey Stoner	AUS	Ducati Marlboro Team	Ducati	44'44.982
2	20	46	Valentino Rossi	ITA	Fiat Yamaha Team	Yamaha	44'50.771
3	16	2	Dani Pedrosa	SPA	Repsol Honda Team	Honda	44'53.329
4	13	5	Colin Edwards	USA	Tech 3 Yamaha	Yamaha	44'57.660
5	11	4	Andrea Dovizioso	ITA	JiR Team Scot MotoGP	Honda	44'59.783
6	10	48	Jorge Lorenzo	SPA	Fiat Yamaha Team	Yamaha	45'00.672
7	9	69	Nicky Hayden	USA	Repsol Honda Team	Honda	45'03.178
8	8	7	Chris Vermeulen	AUS	Rizla Suzuki MotoGP	Suzuki	45'06.648
9	7	56	Shinya Nakano	JPN	San Carlo Honda Gresini	Honda	45'14.336
10	6	13	Anthony West	AUS	Kawasaki Racing Team	Kawasaki	45'26.012
11	5	24	Toni Elias	SPA	Alice Team	Ducati	45'29.408
12	4	14	Randy de Puniet	FRA	LCR Honda MotoGP	Honda	45'31.181
13	3	50	Sylvain Guintoli	FRA	Alice Team	Ducati	45'33.713
14	2	11	Ben Spies	USA	Rizla Suzuki MotoGP	Suzuki	45'34.573
15	1	15	Alex de Angelis	RSM	San Carlo Honda Gresini	Honda	46'07.168
16		33	Marco Melandri	ITA	Ducati Marlboro Team	Ducati	46'15.003
		52	**James Toseland**	**GBR**	**Tech 3 Yamaha**	**Yamaha**	45'32.234
			Not classified				
		21	John Hopkins	USA	Kawasaki Racing Team	Kawasaki	24'18.021

NETHERLANDS

Assen, 28 June

I was determined that I would put on a better and more rewarding show around the Dutch track

carried the dreadful disappointment of Donington Park with me to Holland for the ninth round at Assen, in the north of the country, where I had twice been a winner in WSB. And, try as I might, I just couldn't put to the back of my mind the upset I felt at letting down all those faithful fans, who were just waiting for me to give them something to cheer on my home track.

To say that Donington was a devastating disappointment is probably the understatement of the century. I was determined that I would put on a better and more rewarding show around the Dutch track. But, as it turned out, it did not go quite as I had wanted or expected, and I was left yet again wondering what to do to stop the rot.

The problem was still my setting up of the bike. We just couldn't seem to get it right

I know there are better results in me, but until I get the set-up spot on I am banging my head against a brick wall

OK, I did at least make it into the top ten, but I was planning on a much stronger show than that. But qualifying thirteenth was not much help and I knew when I went to the line for the Saturday afternoon race I had my work cut out to make up places on the other guys.

The problem was still my setting up of the bike. We just couldn't seem to get it right and as a consequence I was suffering and having to try and make up for the machine's deficiencies with some pretty hard riding. That in itself brings its own dangers.

In frustrating contrast, on the other side of the Tech 3 Yamaha garage, my team-mate Colin Edwards appeared to have his bike dialled in very strongly, while I just couldn't achieve the same level. And, despite Colin's willingness to help me with his technical read-outs and ideas, I was still baffled. It was clearly an issue we would have to resolve, otherwise I was going nowhere fast. I know there are better results in me, but until I get the set-up spot on I am banging my head against a brick wall.

I must say, though, that the weather gods have been conspiring against me with ever-changing conditions, giving me little or no time to find the right fix: just when we seemed to have cracked it for the dry it rained, or vice versa and, once again, we were left scratching our heads. Maybe I wasn't getting my message across. Whatever, we needed desperately to get it sorted if I was to get back to a good strong run up the title table.

Right now I am far from comfortable and we have lost a lot of ground on the group ahead of me

After those pleasing top-six finishes at the Italian round in Mugello and the Spanish round in Barcelona – two tracks with real technical issues to master – I was full of confidence for both Donington and Assen, two tracks I knew something about. Well, to my continuing horror, we know what happened at Donington . . .

Assen dawned with fresh hope for me, but it was not to be, despite the fact that I was so fired up to put in a performance that would erase the embarrassment of Donington. I copied Colin's set-up, but it was of little use and I couldn't find any real improvement in the handling or feel of the bike.

I guess time will tell and eventually we'll get the problem worked out and the bike to my liking. But right now I am far from comfortable and we have lost a lot of ground on the group ahead of me. There's no way I am enjoying finishing ninth when I know I am worth a good few places higher than that. It is not that my riding has worsened, and my motivation and determination haven't faltered – it is a crucial technical issue, pure and simple.

I know that I, and the team, have said this year is a learning curve for me, but I don't want to hide behind that as an excuse when all my instincts press me to go one better every time I get out on the track. When your progress comes to a standstill

while the other guys, in contrast, are improving, they shove you back a few places. And without the bike set up effectively it is difficult to do the job to stop them getting away.

We all agreed in the garage to get our heads together for the next round in Germany and I feel I have to put in a really strong effort to get my ideas across. But I am ready, willing and able to listen, discuss and decide what is going to be best to boost my results and get back into the top-six reckonings. As far as my riding is concerned, I'm happy. So is my team boss Herve and my manager Roger.

Roger, incidentally, has been upset at criticisms that he has allowed me, like Lewis Hamilton in Formula One, to become distracted by off-track events, happenings and promotions. Nothing could be more wrong. Like Lewis, I'm sure, I enjoy the peripherals, meeting people and attending functions and playing and singing for the fans. But I don't feel that responsibilities away from racing put pressure on me. In fact, they help me relax. So anybody taking a pop at Roger can think again – they are dead wrong.

Pos	Pts	No	Rider	Nation	Team	Bike	Total time
1	25	1	Casey Stoner	AUS	Ducati Marlboro Team	Ducati	42'12.337
2	20	2	Dani Pedrosa	SPA	Repsol Honda Team	Honda	42'23.647
3	16	5	Colin Edwards	USA	Tech 3 Yamaha	Yamaha	42'29.230
4	13	69	Nicky Hayden	USA	Repsol Honda Team	Honda	42'32.814
5	11	4	Andrea Dovizioso	ITA	JiR Team Scot MotoGP	Honda	42'39.683
6	10	48	Jorge Lorenzo	SPA	Fiat Yamaha Team	Yamaha	42'40.945
7	9	7	Chris Vermeulen	AUS	Rizla Suzuki MotoGP	Suzuki	42'44.667
8	8	56	Shinya Nakano	JPN	San Carlo Honda Gresini	Honda	42'47.229
9	**7**	**52**	**James Toseland**	**GBR**	**Tech 3 Yamaha**	**Yamaha**	**42'50.903**
10	6	50	Sylvain Guintoli	FRA	Alice Team	Ducati	42'51.154
11	5	46	Valentino Rossi	ITA	Fiat Yamaha Team	Yamaha	42'58.362
12	4	24	Toni Elias	SPA	Alice Team	Ducati	43'00.550
13	3	33	Marco Melandri	ITA	Ducati Marlboro Team	Ducati	43'11.931
			Not classified				
		13	Anthony West	AUS	Kawasaki Racing Team	Kawasaki	11'41.383
			Not finished first lap				
		14	Randy de Puniet	FRA	LCR Honda MotoGP	Honda	
		15	Alex de Angelis	RSM	San Carlo Honda Gresini	Honda	

NETHERLANDS
ROUND 9

RESULTS

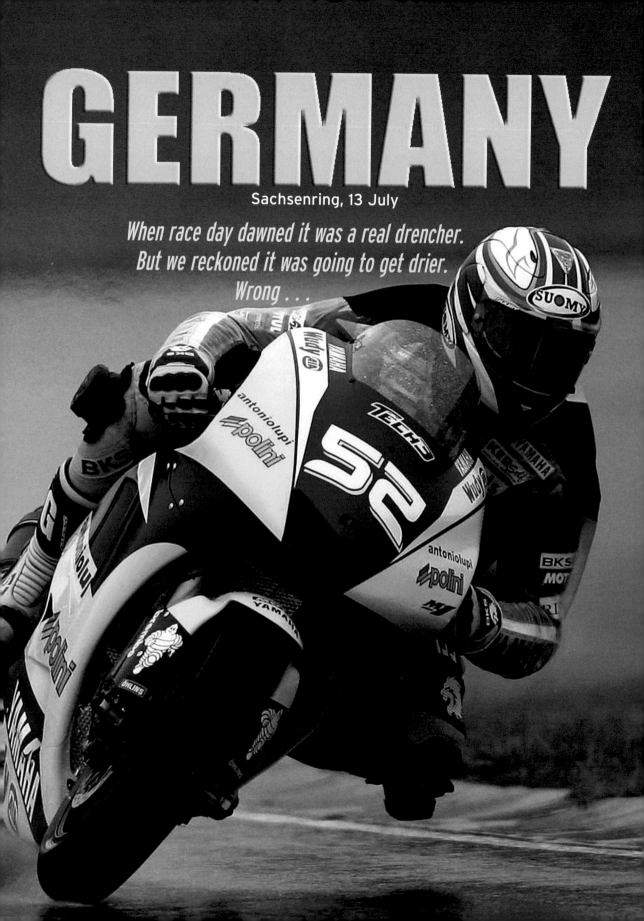

GERMANY

Sachsenring, 13 July

*When race day dawned it was a real drencher.
But we reckoned it was going to get drier.
Wrong . . .*

We opted for a dry-weather setting, and that is what I had to cope with in my first fully wet MotoGP race

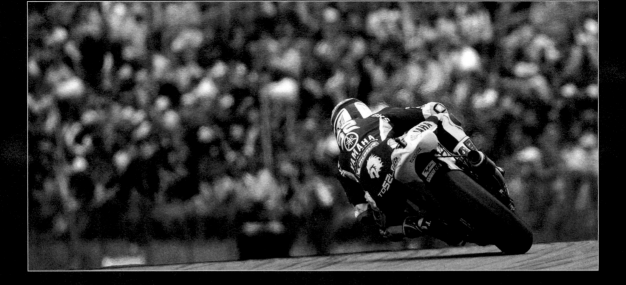

Gambling, as we all know, is something that has led to the downfall of many risk takers. And I am no exception.

In this business, taking risks goes with the territory: squeezing through spaces at 200mph that you would turn sideways to walk through; diving into blind corners flat-out and striving to out-brake an equally committed rival or two at the very last second.

And, of course, tyre choices. Which brings me to my big gamble that went horribly wrong at the Sachsenring for the German GP: the tyres. Or, more precisely, the rear rubber.

I had arrived at the scene of the old East German Grand Prix – in its heyday when it was behind the Iron Curtain, 300,000 spectators used to jam-pack the place – anxious to get my act together after the disappointments of Assen and Donington Park.

But while motivation and a determination to put things right may be admirable qualities to carry you over the humps and bumps of adversity, they are not always the key factors. Sometimes, as was the case in Germany, it is a simpler problem.

After such a promising start to my MotoGP career, I had dropped into a slump that was both irritating and costly, and my frustration at a dreadful run of flops, due in the main to my not being able to get the bike set up properly, was a big concern.

We'd had a so-so build-up and I managed to grab eleventh place on the grid. Not too bad – even though I felt I could have done a bit better.

When race day dawned it was a real drencher. But we reckoned it was going to get drier. Wrong . . .

We opted for a dry-weather setting, and that is what I had to cope with in my first fully wet MotoGP race. The result was that the back-end of the bike was far too stiff and I had hardly any grip at all. That is just what you do not need at 200-plus-mph in a downpour. But that is what I was stuck with and I just had to try and make the best of it as the weather refused to improve.

The irony is that I got off to probably my best start, an absolute flyer, and by the first corner I had made it from eleventh place to fifth and almost fourth.

Under any other circumstances, and with the right setting, that would have been a dream opening and an opportunity to defend my position in the company of the best bike riders in the world. But when Jorge Lorenzo went down big time just in front of me on the same tyre as I had, I told myself to get sensible, hang back and go at a pace appropriate for the unfavourable conditions. My plan was to finish the race as high as I could without risking a spill.

▶ The weather got the better of several riders, including Dani Pedrosa.

The difficult conditions tripped up the
race leader Pedrosa, who fractured
an ankle and a finger

Jorge, having the same problems as me, got niggled and gave his bike a big handful. That was just what it did not need and it responded by high-siding him out of the running. It was a spectacular lesson for me and I decided the safest bet for me now, after that bad, bad gamble, was to settle for the pace I was running at without any more risk than necessary.

I am pleased that I contained myself and raced according to the difficult conditions that tripped up not only Lorenzo but also my teammate Colin Edwards, Marco Melandri and race leader Pedrosa, who fractured an ankle and a finger.

Casey Stoner on the Ducati was a revelation: he just blasted away from the rest of us as if he was on a different track. Valentino Rossi, celebrating an amazing record of 202 consecutive GPs, played it cute and held onto second place. It was enough to give him back the lead in a championship turning into a gripping dog-fight.

I felt that I had learned something from the experience and that at long last I had started to get to grips with the set-up

Bridgestone tyres got a 1-2-3 finish – Chris Vermeulen on a Suzuki was in third place – on a track where they had never even won before.

I dropped down to fourteenth place at one stage and suffered the frustration of being lapped by the two leaders as I struggled to work my way up to eleventh and stay aboard a bike that clearly wanted to pitch me off every time I tried to gas it.

Overall, and despite the continuation of my bad run, I felt that I had learned something from the experience and that at long last I had started to get to grips with the set-up.

I refused to let it get me down and reminded myself that, up until my rotten run began, I'd had six successive top-six finishes and that I had the capability of getting up there again. It was a feeling pressed onto me by both Roger and Herve. I must say my website buzzed with positive messages from loyal fans who, in their hundreds, bothered to take time to boost my ego.

I felt delighted that the next race was to be the US Grand Prix at Laguna Seca, California, one of my favourite tracks from WSB days, and a venue where I had always felt confident.

My prayer was just that it would stay dry with some welcoming California sunshine.

GERMANY ROUND 10

RESULTS

Pos	Pts	No	Rider	Nation	Team	Bike	Total time
1	25	1	Casey Stoner	AUS	Ducati Marlboro Team	Ducati	47'30.057
2	20	46	Valentino Rossi	ITA	Fiat Yamaha Team	Yamaha	47'33.765
3	16	7	Chris Vermeulen	AUS	Rizla Suzuki MotoGP	Suzuki	47'44.059
4	13	15	Alex de Angelis	RSM	San Carlo Honda Gresini	Honda	47'44.181
5	11	4	Andrea Dovizioso	ITA	JiR Team Scot MotoGP	Honda	48'12.079
6	10	50	Sylvain Guintoli	FRA	Alice Team	Ducati	48'16.705
7	9	65	Loris Capirossi	ITA	Rizla Suzuki MotoGP	Suzuki	48'34.540
8	8	14	Randy de Puniet	FRA	LCR Honda MotoGP	Honda	48'34.645
9	7	56	Shinya Nakano	JPN	San Carlo Honda Gresini	Honda	48'46.830
10	6	13	Anthony West	AUS	Kawasaki Racing Team	Kawasaki	48'59.332
11	**5**	**52**	**James Toseland**	**GBR**	**Tech 3 Yamaha**	**Yamaha**	**47'41.757**
12	4	24	Toni Elias	SPA	Alice Team	Ducati	47'43.954
13	3	69	Nicky Hayden	USA	Repsol Honda Team	Honda	48'13.749
			Not classified				
		5	Colin Edwards	USA	Tech 3 Yamaha	Yamaha	32'10.373
		33	Marco Melandri	ITA	Ducati Marlboro Team	Ducati	14'50.161
		2	Dani Pedrosa	SPA	Repsol Honda Team	Honda	8'05.615
		48	Jorge Lorenzo	SPA	Fiat Yamaha Team	Yamaha	3'23.795

UNITED STATES

Laguna Seca, 20 July

I had high hopes for the race at Laguna Seca,
a track I really enjoy

I honestly fancied my chances of a podium finish and was determined to make the American round the scene of some overdue success

had high hopes for the race at Laguna Seca, a track I really enjoy, but these were thrown into disarray, largely due to a problem with the selection and supply of tyres.

I honestly fancied my chances of a podium finish and was determined to make the American round the scene of some overdue success. But it was not to be, and it was certainly no fault of mine.

The choice of tyre turned out to be a costly misjudgement. Michelin used data from last year's race at the California circuit to build tyres for this year's event – and they got it wrong, so much so that they were profuse in their apologies to me and the whole team, who had worked so hard to give me a bike to do a good job.

The problem was that they brought a range of tyres that were far too hard: we used the softest they had for the race and it only operated at 125°C when we would normally expect a tyre to start working at 140°C. The Hondas always run a slightly harder tyre than Yamaha, so they were able to get the same tyre that we had to work OK for them.

It was pretty evident to us that, whatever I did and however hard I rode in the race, the tyres were not going to behave the way we needed them to, and I was destined to spend my time either right on the edge, or certainly close to it, and on my backside in the gravel if I wasn't careful.

That was Jorge Lorenzo's fate in the first lap of the race, when he unwisely took one chance too many and tried to do the impossible on an unforgivingly hard tyre like mine, and high-sided spectacularly out of yet another race.

That was a vivid lesson for me. And I decided to keep to a pace where I reckoned I could be a finisher under the flag and not in a gravel trap. It was a really disappointing situation because my firm belief, even before I flew into the US, was that I could make it onto the podium. I was confident that I was getting on good terms with the bike, the boys in the garage and Herve, and we were gelling nicely into the sort of unit where I feel comfortably at home.

The first session in Laguna revealed the tyre problem, not only for me but for several other guys, too, and I dropped down to sixteenth fastest, a massive 2.117 seconds slower than Casey Stoner. In the second I fell off along with Ben Spies and Anthony West at turn three. I wasn't happy, as I told Herve, and I wasn't doing the lap times I'd been expecting because I was struggling with the grip.

In qualifying, on the softest tyre we could dig out, I clocked a really pleasing 1.21.848 and held third place until the final two minutes, when I was pushed back to fifth fastest, my best grid since Qatar. I missed a place on the front row by only 0.4 seconds. But I knew it was going to be tough. I'd had to pin it and it wasn't easy, but I'd got the job done and I showed I had the pace.

Furthermore, I was getting the hang of the start and I wasn't nearly as nervous as I had been previously. It is quite a technique to get these MotoGP bikes off the line. When you are flat out at 14,000 revs and you want to dump the clutch as fast as you can, you really need to know what you are doing.

Whatever I did and however hard I rode in the race, the tyres were not going to behave the way we needed them to

I got it dead right in the race. And by the first corner I was in third place with a fantastic start. Not that it lasted long and I had a really hard and prolonged dice with Shinya Nakano hanging onto seventh place, as the other guys piled by me on better-serving tyres than mine.

We knew before the off that it was going to be tough, and when Lorenzo went down his crash only served to remind me how dodgy this race was. But I really did give it my all – or as much as I dared without following Lorenzo over the handlebars.

Towards the end, when I was battling with de Puniet and just trying to block other guys by riding a defensive race, the rear tyre started giving me big, big problems. As hard as I worked, I could not hold off guys who had been my chasers, and seventh place gave way to ninth when Toni Elias and Ben Spies passed me two laps from the end.

Up front, between Valentino Rossi and Casey Stoner, the race had been a blinder, the best for years. And I would love to have been the third party in that squabble. But it was not to be – not just yet, anyway.

Herve and Roger were pleased with my performance under the circumstances, but inwardly I felt that I'd been riding round rather than racing and that's not what I am on the scene to do. I'm not out for the easy option. It is against all my instincts. And disappointment is always hard to swallow when the issue is out of your own hands and your progress is hampered and compounded by somebody else's error.

We'd had a couple of really disappointing races, mainly because of the tyre problems, and I left Laguna praying that the issue would be sorted for Brno, next time out.

There is a strong rumour there will be a one-make tyre rule for next season – and it would be a shame if a company of Michelin's reputation and stature lost the opportunity to stay in racing because of this situation.

In fairness, after an embarrassing weekend for them, they took time to apologise to me and the team. I know we at Tech 3 are capable of a lot more and that is why Laguna was so frustrating. We should, and could, have done a whole lot better.

Towards the end, the rear tyre started giving me big, big problems

UNITED STATES ROUND 11

RESULTS

Pos	Pts	No	Rider	Nation	Team	Bike	Total time
1	25	46	Valentino Rossi	ITA	Fiat Yamaha Team	Yamaha	44'04.311
2	20	1	Casey Stoner	AUS	Ducati Marlboro Team	Ducati	44'17.312
3	16	7	Chris Vermeulen	AUS	Rizla Suzuki MotoGP	Suzuki	44'30.920
4	13	4	Andrea Dovizioso	ITA	JiR Team Scot MotoGP	Honda	44'39.212
5	11	69	Nicky Hayden	USA	Repsol Honda Team	Honda	44'39.974
6	10	14	Randy de Puniet	FRA	LCR Honda MotoGP	Honda	44'41'979
7	9	24	Toni Elias	SPA	Alice Team	Ducati	44'45.940
8	8	11	Ben Spies	USA	Rizla Suzuki MotoGP	Suzuki	44'46.238
9	7	52	**James Toseland**	GBR	Tech 3 Yamaha	Yamaha	44'47.330
10	6	56	Shinya Nakano	JPN	San Carlo Honda Gresini	Honda	44'48.702
11	5	12	Jamie Hacking	USA	Kawasaki Racing Team	Kawasaki	44'50'569
12	4	50	Sylvain Guintoli	FRA	Alice Team	Ducati	44'59.583
13	3	15	Alex de Angelis	RSM	San Carlo Honda Gresini	Honda	44'59.832
14	2	5	Colin Edwards	USA	Tech 3 Yamaha	Yamaha	45'06.691
15	1	64	Loris Capirossi	ITA	Rizla Suzuki MotoGP	Suzuki	45'12.518
16		33	Marco Melandri	ITA	Ducati Marlboro Team	Ducati	45'15.273
		13	Anthony West	AUS	Kawasaki Racing Team	Kawasaki	44'34.872
Not finished first lap							
		48	Jorge Lorenzo	SPA	Fiat Yamaha Team	Yamaha	

CZECH REPUBLIC

Automotodrom Brno, 17 August

On the first four laps I bet I had my elbow scraping the ground half-a-dozen times

I was never in with the slightest hope of troubling the top ten — and I reckon I was pretty lucky to make it back to the garage in one piece

I went to Brno for the Czech Republic Grand Prix – round twelve – full of hope and expectation that, in the three-week lay-off, the tyre problem would have been resolved and I would be given a chance to improve on my results and get somewhere nearer the first and second places I had scored on this track in WSB.

But to my intense irritation, shared I am sure by several other guys, there had been no progress whatsoever. And my entire weekend was a highly forgettable wreck, through no fault of my own.

The utter frustration that downs you when you are striving to give it your all in a race when the equipment is not performing to your expectations is indescribable, and no matter how many apologies are forthcoming, you are left with the conclusion that somebody is not doing their job properly.

I prefer to always get on with the job as best I can, despite whatever setbacks I face, and I am not a natural moaner. But when your crucial contact with the road at speeds close to 200mph is as unpredictably dicey as it was in Brno, there is some justification for complaining.

The whole miserable experience began in atrocious weather when I slid off, and both I and my fellow rookie Jorge Lorenzo failed to register an acceptable time in qualifying and were, initially, out of the race. However, some good sense prevailed, and we were allowed to start from the back of the grid. Not that it helped my mood. I knew I was in for a titanic struggle just to stay on the tarmac and in the race, as was my partner Colin Edwards, who had been a regular front runner.

I somehow limped home in thirteenth place – a place and 10 seconds up on Colin, gaining the two hardest points I have ever earned in racing. The whole experience was a nightmare. It was little compensation that I was the third fastest Michelin rider to complete the race, with Andrea Dovizioso and Lorenzo ahead of me.

Valentino Rossi – on Bridgestone tyres – won after Casey Stoner took a tumble with fifteen laps to go. None of that was in my sight: I was simply battling to stay aboard. Talk about a learning curve! I was never in with the slightest hope of troubling the top ten – and I reckon I was pretty lucky to make it back to the garage in one piece.

I have to confess that my morale has taken a bit of a battering in my fade-out after such a promising start to my MotoGP career.

On the first four laps I bet I had my elbow scraping the ground half-a-dozen times. I have never ridden in conditions anything like that before and I was picking the bike up off the floor all over the place. It was dreadful – a serious problem.

The upshot was that I have dropped out of the top ten without being able to do anything about it – and unless the tyre situation improves I can't see a way back. And that is a serious threat to my reputation and, therefore, my career. Mercifully, my manager Herve is well aware of the problems that have beset me and Colin in the Tech 3 Yamaha team.

I told him that I am doing my utmost to keep my head up high and not to let the issue of the tyres get me down or shatter my confidence. It is, after all, out of my hands. There are six rounds to go and, I guess, a lot of things can still change.

We are a good team with a great bike and we just cannot afford to be finishing at the arse-end of the field. At the start of the season, Colin was on the podium and I was putting in some good results as a first-timer at this level. Then it all changed and only because of the tyres.

There are six rounds to go and, I guess, a lot of things can still change.

It was only after Michelin race boss
Jean-Philippe Weber's assurances
that we were not at risk and the
tyres would not explode that
Colin and I agreed to race

Colin made his position clear when he said: 'The front tyre was crap and it was tearing. It was terrible. The Michelin guys told me there would be no safety issue, it was just a wear problem. But I was going down the straight and the bike was vibrating like crazy.

'Every lap it got worse. The right side of the rear tyre was gone and I couldn't get on the gas. I have never seen a rear tyre as bad as mine and at 180mph it scared the life out of me. I feel so demoralised right now.'

Colin, like me, is not a moaner. So his description of what was happening to him must be taken seriously. It was only after Michelin race boss Jean-Philippe Weber's assurances to all six of his riders that we were not at risk and the tyres would not explode that Colin and I agreed to race.

◄ Casey Stoner took a tumble with fifteen laps to go.

Even Dani Pedrosa, normally so shy and quiet, was moved to have an outspoken pop at the French tyre company: 'They don't recognise their mistakes – they are arrogant. My bike was unrideable. It was the worst race of my career. I felt impotent and ashamed. I was slower than the 250s and that is a very big embarrassment.'

Laguna Seca was humiliating enough, when Nicky Hayden, Colin and I were left struggling, but Brno was the absolute pits. To add to the mystery, Michelin had tested at the resurfaced Brno track in mid-June.

Jean-Philippe Weber admitted they were worried. 'We had a technical lack of performance at the Sachsenring and at Laguna we were way too conservative,' he confessed.

And he promised: 'We will do everything we can. We can do better. We have to speed up our development process.'

He can say that again!

Pos	Pts	No	Rider	Nation	Team	Bike	Total time
1	25	46	Valentino Rossi	ITA	Fiat Yamaha Team	Yamaha	43'28.841
2	20	24	Toni Elias	SPA	Alice Team	Ducati	43'43.845
3	16	64	Loris Capirossi	ITA	Rizla Suzuki MotoGP	Suzuki	43'50.530
4	13	56	Shinya Nakano	JPN	San Carlo Honda Gresini	Honda	43'54.700
5	11	13	Anthony West	AUS	Kawasaki Racing Team	Kawasaki	43'58.306
6	10	7	Chris Vermeulen	AUS	Rizla Suzuki MotoGP	Suzuki	43'59.449
7	9	33	Marco Melandri	ITA	Ducati Marlboro Team	Ducati	44'05.294
8	8	15	Alex de Angelis	RSM	San Carlo Honda Gresini	Honda	44'05.591
9	7	4	Andrea Dovizioso	ITA	JiR Team Scot MotoGP	Honda	44'07.663
10	6	48	Jorge Lorenzo	SPA	Fiat Yamaha Team	Yamaha	44'08.414
11	5	21	John Hopkins	USA	Kawasaki Racing Team	Kawasaki	44'08.451
12	4	50	Sylvain Guintoli	FRA	Alice Team	Ducati	44'09.733
13	3	52	**James Toseland**	GBR	Tech 3 Yamaha	Yamaha	44'40.331
14	2	5	Colin Edwards	USA	Tech 3 Yamaha	Yamaha	44'49.974
15	1	2	Dani Pedrosa	SPA	Repsol Honda Team	Honda	45'05.879
16		14	Randy de Puniet	FRA	LCR Honda MotoGP	Honda	45'07'248
			Not classified				
		1	Casey Stoner	AUS	Ducati Marlboro Team	Ducati	11'49.228

CZECH REPUBLIC
ROUND 12

RESULTS

I would like to take this opportunity to express my profound sadness at the death of Craig Jones after his crash at Brands Hatch. He was one of my best friends – and a brilliant rider who was destined for a lot of success. I rode the Brno race wearing a black armband and carried his number 18 on my fairing as a mark of my respect for a great lad.

SAN MARINO

Misano, 31 August

*It felt brilliant: I was on great form
and giving it everything with some really hard-to-beat
guys all wanting my bit of track*

After the mishaps and mess-ups, caused mainly by the tyre problems, it was a relief to get back to where I felt I belonged, right into the front-running fray at Misano.

I have to confess – as I guess most Michelin runners would do – that the disappointment and utter frustration I was feeling after a miserable run of results was really getting to me. And it would be too easy for outsiders, not really aware of the issues, to wrongly believe I was making excuses to cover a loss of form. Nothing could have been further from the truth and I flew into Italy hell-bent on putting on a show to floor the sceptics.

It is difficult to explain how maddening a situation it can be when you are doing your best, and sticking your neck out, to find a way round a problem only to have it mercilessly track you and trap you at just about every turn on the racetrack.

From my point of view, and there is no big-headedness here, I know I am better than I may have been seen to be, particularly by people who are not in a position to realise or understand the tremendous problems I was facing with the tyres. But if motivation could be the password to open a fresh challenge then that is what I carried with me to Misano – and, thank God, it worked and got me firmly back on track after a series of setbacks that might, had I not stayed optimistic, have ruined my hopes.

Michelin, too, had worked really hard to resurrect their reputation and gave us some rubber that was much better than the stuff they had given us previously – which had led to such a disastrous outcome.

It was a red-hot day in Misano in more ways than one – with blazing 35-degree sunshine and a fiercely fired-up posse of guys around me, all given to the idea that if a win, beating Valentino Rossi and Casey Stoner, was not on the cards then the follow-up places, and maybe a podium, were certainly up for grabs.

At one stage it seemed odds-on that I was on for a fifth place – that would have been my best-ever MotoGP finish – having stuck it to Andrea Dovizioso and Shinya Nakano in a really tough shoulder-to-shoulder battle. But six laps from the flag I dropped back to sixth. It was a hell of a job to keep Loris Capirossi and Dovi at bay in the closing stages, but somehow I managed it, even though grip on the rear end was near zilch.

It was a relief to get back to where I felt I belonged, right into the front-running fray at Misano

I had got off to a really good start from ninth on the grid and got into the game pleasingly quickly: when I passed Dovizioso at about the halfway mark he started having troubles and so did I, but I made the pass stick OK.

Chris Vermeulen overtook me near the end and cleared off and that was a bit niggling because I felt sure I was going to grab fifth place. But I didn't have the same safe level of grip that he had.

I must say it still felt brilliant: I was on great form and giving it everything with some really hard-to-beat guys all wanting my bit of track. I really enjoyed the challenge and the competition.

From my standpoint, I thought, this is what I am here for, and I made my bike about ten-feet wide . . . probably the widest Yamaha in racing history. I was determined in my plan to make sure they could not get by. I realised both Loris and Andrea wanted my place and were ready to really go for it in front of their home fans. The rear tyre was a goner by then and I was sliding all over the place for the last four laps, but it did nothing to wreck my determination to hang onto my sixth place.

*I stuck it to Andrea Dovizioso
and Shinya Nakano in a really tough
shoulder-to-shoulder battle*

The big problem was that I could not get any lean angle, and that is a serious issue. With a lack of torque you can't just dive in, stop it and fire it out of the corners. When you are down a couple of k's mid-corner, you can lose momentum when you reach the straight and end up being passed.

Loris did manage to squeeze by on the last-but-one lap, but I blocked him and he had to go wide and that left me just enough room to get him back. It was close. Very close. But I didn't touch him, so it was all fair and square.

On the last two laps I blocked the corners and made sure sixth place was not going to be snatched from me. I had the biggest, scariest front-end slide of my career, a real nerve-wracker, on a fast right on the last lap, but there was no way I was going to back off or yield an inch.

Overall, I have to say, Michelin had knuckled down to sorting out the problems and, though they have had a lot of stick – deservedly so at times – they got their act together in Italy. And so did I.

'It was a fantastic race by James – and I am really pleased to see him back up there fighting as we know he can do' HERVE PONCHARAL

Herve was delighted, and he said afterwards: 'It was a fantastic race by James – and I am really pleased to see him back up there fighting as we know he can do.

'When he suffers, so does the whole team. But he has never let his head drop even though it has not been an easy spell for him. He has given our team, Yamaha and Michelin, 100 per cent.

'This result has given him a big boost for the remainder of the season – and maybe a podium is not impossible before the end.'

I couldn't have put it better myself.

Pos	Pts	No	Rider	Nation	Team	Bike	Total time
1	25	46	Valentino Rossi	ITA	Fiat Yamaha Team	Yamaha	44'41.884
2	20	48	Jorge Lorenzo	SPA	Fiat Yamaha Team	Yamaha	44'45.047
3	16	24	Toni Elias	SPA	Alice Team	Ducati	44'53.589
4	13	2	Dani Pedrosa	SPA	Repsol Honda Team	Honda	44'59.354
5	11	7	Chris Vermeulen	AUS	Rizla Suzuki MotoGP	Suzuki	45'05.293
6	10	52	James Toseland	GBR	Tech 3 Yamaha	Yamaha	45'08.092
7	9	64	Loris Capirossi	ITA	Rizla Suzuki MotoGP	Suzuki	45'08.708
8	8	4	Andrea Dovizioso	ITA	JiR Team Scot MotoGP	Honda	45'09.475
9	7	33	Marco Melandri	ITA	Ducati Marlboro Team	Ducati	45'15.053
10	6	5	Colin Edwards	USA	Tech 3 Yamaha	Yamaha	45'18.413
11	5	50	Sylvain Guintoli	FRA	Alice Team	Ducati	45'23.965
12	4	56	Shinya Nakano	JPN	San Carlo Honda Gresini	Honda	45'25.692
13	3	13	Anthony West	AUS	Kawasaki Racing Team	Kawasaki	45'36.759
14	2	21	John Hopkins	USA	Kawasaki Racing Team	Kawasaki	45'37.038
			Not classified				
		1	Casey Stoner	AUS	Ducati Marlboro Team	Ducati	11'11.968
		15	Alex de Angelis	RSM	San Carlo Honda Gresini	Honda	1'46.395
			Not starting				
		69	Nicky Hayden	USA	Repsol Honda Team	Honda	
			Not finished first lap				
		14	Randy de Puniet	FRA	LCR Honda MotoGP	Honda	

SAN MARINO ROUND 13

RESULTS

INDIANAPOLIS

Indianapolis, 14 September

*I arrived at Indianapolis full of hope,
but the weather clearly wasn't on my side*

I was relaxed enough to do a gig with the Indianapolis Symphony Orchestra, which followed a promotional visit to Las Vegas

If ever a race was best forgotten it was this inaugural outing at the historic Indianapolis track – the Brickyard. It was, for me, a top-to-bottom total write-off with an embarrassing eighteenth and second-to-last finish.

I could not get away from the place soon enough, but even that proved difficult in the dreadful weather – my plane back to England was cancelled and I had to hang around for another night in Chicago.

The race was a disaster, due mainly to my own mistake when I opted for the wrong tyres in worsening conditions, the trailing aftermath of Hurricane Ike and its accompanying gales and torrents of rain.

I had arrived full of hope and happy at the prospect of taking on yet another circuit I didn't know, a fact which also applied to all the other guys. I was relaxed enough even to do a gig with the Indianapolis Symphony Orchestra, and that followed on from a promotional visit to Las Vegas on behalf of Yamaha, with Valentino Rossi and my teammate Colin Edwards.

I made my start aggressive, and by lap five I was in eighth place and hanging on in there

But whatever joy I got out of all this off-track stuff was very quickly swept away by the tidal conditions that made the race a risky challenge. In truth, I put the skids under my own chances with a setting that was too soft.

It was initially OK and felt pretty good. I didn't get off the line too well, but I made my start aggressive, with a forceful ride around the outside into turn one, and passed a few people. I have to say I felt pretty good and confident, and by lap five I was in eighth place and hanging on in there.

From then on in, with the track drying off in unpredictable blasts of wind that threatened to blow us all into the gravel, it was a complete nightmare. I was sliding backwards down the field on the wrong tyres for the changing conditions, unable to do a thing to put it right. But there was nobody to blame but myself. Everybody else got faster as the track dried, but I was in really deep trouble and could not go any faster. The back wheel was spinning and, clearly, I was a bit too soft with the back-end setting. When it started raining again I found a bit of pace once more and managed to do similar times to the guys up front, but by that time I had lost loads of places and it turned into a useless exercise.

Colin, too, had his problems and only managed to secure fifteenth place in what was a forgettable outing for our Tech 3 team.

I will never forget the gales. They kept changing direction and were totally unpredictable. You'd come to a corner expecting the wind to be the same as it was the lap before, and it'd be blowing in another direction altogether. It made the situation hairy as hell. I guess we were all relieved that race director Paul Butler called the race off before somebody got hurt.

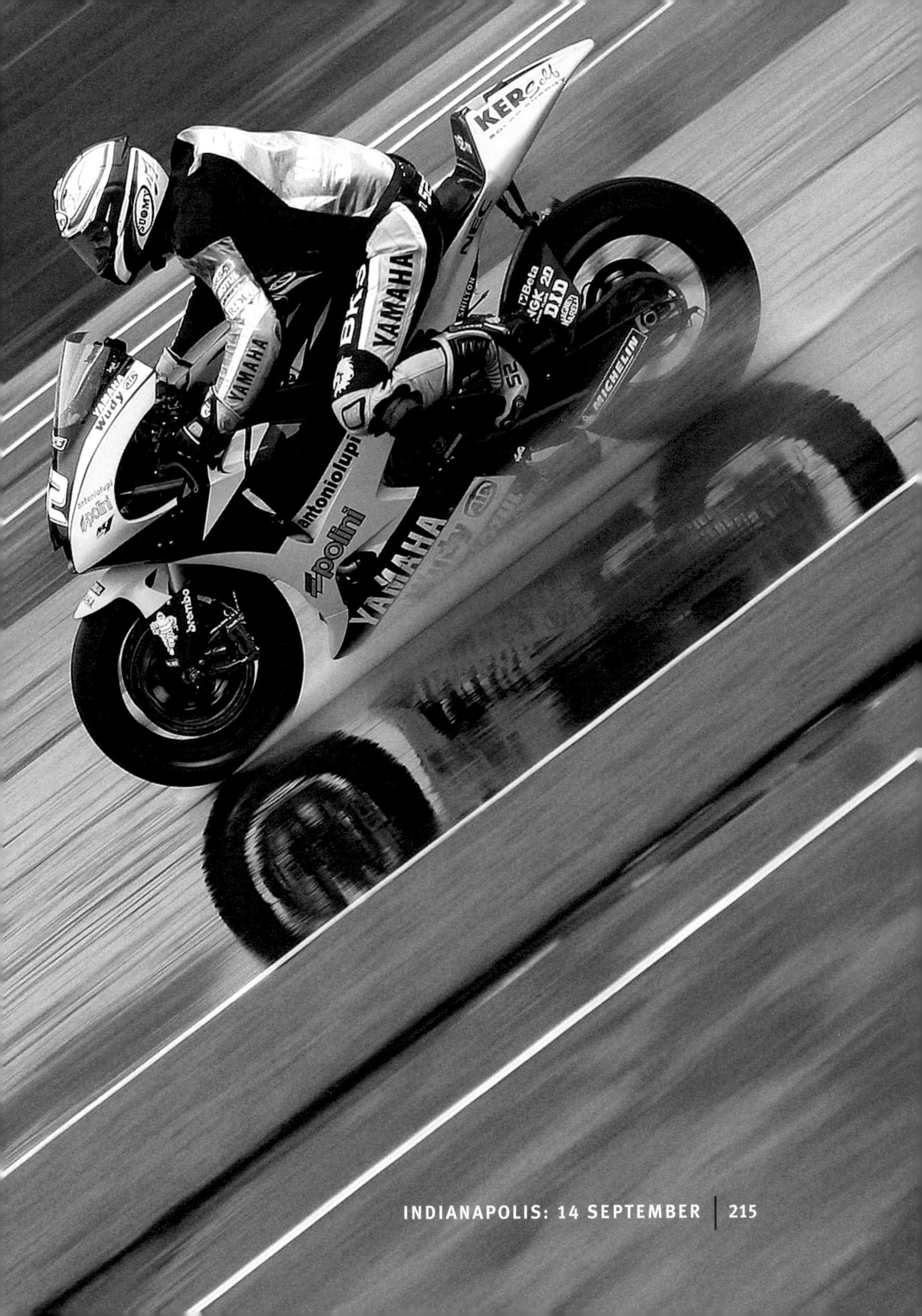
YAMAHA
BKS
antoniolupi
polini
YAMAHA
MICHELIN
brembo
52

With Japan and Motegi coming up next, and the countdown really starting on my first season, I am determined to hit that top-six mark again

It was not even a learning curve for me as so many other races had been in my rookie season: I came away none the wiser about anything, except not to get too downhearted when things went wrong.

Herve was not too pleased. Afterwards he said: 'I am very disappointed. James started quite well but he lost a lot of ground while Colin was again very cautious in the first laps like Misano.

'When we remember what we were doing in the first part of the season and we see what we are doing now I am not very happy. And we have to find some solutions because we should not be finishing where we are.'

The setbacks we were suffering were further highlighted by Valentino's remarkable success. It was at this race that he passed legend Giacomo Agostini's long-standing record of wins – a fantastic achievement from a brilliant rider and a thoroughly likeable guy.

With Japan and Motegi coming up next, and the countdown really starting on my first season, I am determined to hit that top-six mark again. I am just praying that the weather isn't up to its usual wet tricks, throwing me and the team into any confusion about settings, and I can settle down to a race without problems and show what I can really do.

Pos	Pts	No	Rider	Nation	Team	Bike	Total time
1	25	46	Valentino Rossi	ITA	Fiat Yamaha Team	Yamaha	37'20.095
2	20	69	Nicky Hayden	USA	Repsol Honda Team	Honda	37'26.067
3	16	48	Jorge Lorenzo	SPA	Fiat Yamaha Team	Yamaha	37'27.953
4	13	1	Casey Stoner	AUS	Ducati Marlboro Team	Ducati	37'48.257
5	11	4	Andrea Dovizioso	ITA	JiR Team Scot MotoGP	Honda	37'48.919
6	10	11	Ben Spies	USA	Rizla Suzuki MotoGP	Suzuki	37'49.740
7	9	50	Sylvain Guintoli	FRA	Alice Team	Ducati	37'56.318
8	8	2	Dani Pedrosa	SPA	Repsol Honda Team	Honda	37'57.353
9	7	7	Chris Vermeulen	AUS	Rizla Suzuki MotoGP	Suzuki	37'58.537
10	6	15	Alex de Angelis	RSM	San Carlo Honda Gresini	Honda	38'02.532
11	5	13	Anthony West	AUS	Kawasaki Racing Team	Kawasaki	38'07.274
12	4	24	Toni Elias	SPA	Alice Team	Ducati	38'16.057
13	3	14	Randy de Puniet	FRA	LCR Honda MotoGP	Honda	38'17.461
14	2	21	John Hopkins	USA	Kawasaki Racing Team	Kawasaki	38'18.448
15	1	5	Colin Edwards	USA	Tech 3 Yamaha	Yamaha	38'20.708
16		64	Loris Capirossi	ITA	Rizla Suzuki MotoGP	Suzuki	38'25.715
17		56	Shinya Nakano	JPN	San Carlo Honda Gresini	Honda	38'25.949
18		52	James Toseland	GBR	Tech 3 Yamaha	Yamaha	38'28.063
19		33	Marco Melandri	ITA	Ducati Marlboro Team	Ducati	38'41.118

INDIANAPOLIS ROUND 14

RESULTS

JAPAN

Motegi, 28 September

I was locked in a real battle with John Hopkins for most of the race

he Twin Ring Motegi circuit north of Tokyo was the scene of the Japanese Grand Prix, round fifteen of a championship that was potentially about to become a historic one. My fellow Yamaha rider Valentino Rossi was hoping to secure his eighth world title with an incredible 98th GP career win, and establish himself as probably the greatest rider of all time.

Nearly 58,000 fans turned up for the 24-lap chase that was, for me, another challenging and hard-fought battle. I was happy enough that in qualifying I was tenth quickest, only 1.3 seconds behind Jorge Lorenzo on pole. And what with him and Nicky Hayden lining up on the front row of the grid on their Michelins, I started with plenty of confidence that the rubber should be OK.

From lights-out Stoner, desperate to defend his title, and Rossi went for it and cleared off. The rest of us dropped in behind to settle our own personal differences. And I had a total nail-biter of a race with John Hopkins.

We were locked in a real battle for most of the race and I managed to keep him at bay for a long time, giving it my absolute all. I was pleased that, however hard the dice was, I didn't make any mistakes: I was consistent, well in control and ready to mix it with John if he fancied the challenge. And he did!

I was up with Colin Edwards and Shinya Nakano early on, but I had been playing with the rear shock all weekend to try and get more grip at full lean angle. Although it was the best it had been, I was still losing loads of time on the exits and they started pulling away from me. Not by much – but enough to keep me out of the equation.

It is such a stop–start circuit that you need to exit the corners really strongly. If you can do that you can pull a couple of tenths a lap.

I was satisfied that I could not have done any more or ridden any harder

Hopkins got so close to me that his shoulder pushed my clutch lever in and it disengaged, leaving me briefly out of gear

I really wanted tenth place, but my problem with the shock hampered me and cost me time. Then I had a really bizarre setback. Hopkins decided to go for it. He dived under me at turn one on the last lap. I tried to pass him back down the straight, but he came back at me and got so close that, when he came across me, his shoulder pushed my clutch lever in and it disengaged and left me briefly out of gear. But with the tightness of the scrap we were having that was all the advantage, however small, he needed, and he pulled away. I gave chase and tried all I could to get him back, but he didn't put a foot wrong for what was left of the lap.

It was really disappointing to lose the place I had so successfully defended so close to the finish, but I was satisfied that I could not have done any more or ridden any harder.

Herve was obviously in agreement when he said: 'James rode a really strong race and fought very hard . . . as always.

'It was yet another hard weekend for him on his first time at this track. But he gave his maximum.'

The frustration at being held back by lack of familiarity with a race track, especially when I'm all fired up and bursting to do well, is difficult to get across to people who can only watch and wonder what is keeping me off the podium.

But I left Motegi content that my commitment had been as strong as possible and was looking forward to the Australian circuit, which I know so well.

Maybe, just maybe, with my increasing confidence in the bike and its improved performance, along with racing on a track I know and on which I have been successful, I can pull a podium out of the bag. It will not be for want of trying and giving it my all.

I'm looking forward to the next round in Australia,
a circuit I know so well

Pos	Pts	No	Rider	Nation	Team	Bike	Total time
1	25	46	Valentino Rossi	ITA	Fiat Yamaha Team	Yamaha	43'09.599
2	20	1	Casey Stoner	AUS	Ducati Marlboro Team	Ducati	43'11.542
3	16	2	Dani Pedrosa	SPA	Repsol Honda Team	Honda	43'14.465
4	13	48	Jorge Lorenzo	SPA	Fiat Yamaha Team	Yamaha	43'15.764
5	11	69	Nicky Hayden	USA	Repsol Honda Team	Honda	43'34.192
6	10	64	Loris Capirossi	ITA	Rizla Suzuki MotoGP	Suzuki	43'35.284
7	9	5	Colin Edwards	USA	Tech 3 Yamaha	Yamaha	43'35.517
8	8	56	Shinya Nakano	JPN	San Carlo Honda Gresini	Honda	43'35.602
9	7	4	Andrea Dovizioso	ITA	JiR Team Scot MotoGP	Honda	43'35.818
10	6	21	John Hopkins	USA	Kawasaki Racing Team	Kawasaki	43'46.730
11	5	52	James Toseland	GBR	Tech 3 Yamaha	Yamaha	43'47.173
12	4	14	Randy de Puniet	FRA	LCR Honda MotoGP	Honda	43'47.619
13	3	33	Marco Melandri	ITA	Ducati Marlboro Team	Ducati	43'49.367
14	2	50	Sylvain Guintoli	FRA	Alice Team	Ducati	43'55.445
15	1	13	Anthony West	AUS	Kawasaki Racing Team	Kawasaki	44'05.347
16		24	Toni Elias	SPA	Alice Team	Ducati	44'08.919
		15	Alex de Angelis	RSM	San Carlo Honda Gresini	Honda	44'21.997
Not classified							
		7	Chris Vermeulen	AUS	Rizla Suzuki MotoGP	Suzuki	29'15.997
Not finished first lap							
		64	Kousuke Akiyoshi	JPN	Rizla Suzuki MotoGP	Suzuki	

AUSTRALIA

Phillip Island, 5 October

This was a race to remember for all the right reasons!

I was confident that being on familiar ground at long last could only benefit me and the team

The race at Phillip Island for the Australian Grand Prix was my toughest and most tense race so far. I am hopeful that whatever doubts anybody may have had about my skill and ability as a rider were wiped out by my all-out effort. Certainly, any doubts I'd had myself in the build-up to this race were dispelled by forty-five minutes of ballsy racing. This was a race to remember for all the right reasons!

Having already had some pleasing test and race outings at Phillip Island – a first and second in WSB the year before – I was confident that being on familiar ground at long last could only benefit me and the team, especially if the weather stayed dry. And that's just the way it worked out.

I felt right on top of the job from the word go, and a fifth place on the grid, the middle of row two, was a bit disappointing. I was planning for better. When I checked the times after qualifying, I found I was just 0.366 seconds off pole – I missed a front row place by only 0.2 seconds. Going wide at the second corner and a bit of a slide robbed me of the split second that would have put me up with Stoner and Hayden. But it seemed to me that a podium to celebrate my twenty-eighth birthday in the best possible way was definitely not out of the question.

▼ I hoped to celebrate my birthday with a strong performance at Phillip Island.

*I was just 0.366 seconds off pole — I missed
a front row place by only 0.2 seconds*

I couldn't wait for the race, and the misery I had suffered before due to a mixture of bad weather, dodgy tyres and unfamiliar circuits was all forgotten. I felt hopeful again that I could make my presence felt in this race.

Some minor adjustments to the settings, when the practice day rain gave way to lovely dry weather, enabled me to go to the line with the bike as I wanted it to be. I was excited at the prospect of being able to push without the wheels spinning and sending the bike sideways.

At the start of the race, Stoner and Hayden belted off into the distance. I ended up being locked in what turned out to be the battle of the race, a real spectacular for the entire 27 laps, with Lorenzo, Dovizioso and Nakano. And then Rossi, who'd had a crash in qualifying and was twelfth on the grid, came into play when he carved his way through the field with his usual brilliance and commitment.

I got into third place from the start, surrendered it briefly to Lorenzo on lap three, but grabbed it back on the first turn on lap five. And that set up a race-long tussle, a real breath taker which must have been thrilling for anybody watching.

When Rossi joined in I managed to keep him behind me for six laps. He passed me twice, but I got him back straightaway. I can't explain what a fantastic feeling that was – me passing the multi-champ when he was on a charge!

When Valentino set off after Stoner and Hayden, I lost touch with him but there were still three other guys to contend with. By now my back tyre was going off a wee bit. But there was nothing I could do to preserve it without surrendering the position I had worked so hard to achieve.

Two laps from the end, just when it looked as if I would clinch fourth – which would have been fantastic and my best finish in MotoGP – the rear end was spinning and I lost a crucial bit of grip. As a result I got overtaken by Lorenzo and Dovizioso.

I knew fourth place was up for grabs so I had a go at Dovizioso at Honda Hairpin on the last lap, a move he didn't like and later had a bit of a moan about, but I ran wide. I didn't touch him though and he got upset for nothing. If he had done the same to me I would have accepted it as part and parcel of the job, especially as I was just trying to do my best and fighting for the best result of my MotoGP career.

When Rossi joined in I managed to keep him behind me for six laps. He passed me twice, but I got him back straightaway

Nakano got through as I went wide, but I passed him back at Siberia, only for him to come under me when I overdid it again.

I was bitterly disappointed that I didn't finish higher, even on the podium, but I was delighted with the way I rode, even if Dovizioso did describe me somewhat unfairly as being 'dangerous'.

Rossi, who made it into second place, was full of praise for my effort and my showdown with him. He said, 'James rode really well – and he certainly took me by surprise. Twice.' He also said of my racing, 'He rides like a devil, he rides like his life is depending on it'.

The boys in the garage, too, were as pleased for me as I was for myself. And Herve definitely made me blush when he said, 'James was absolutely incredible and he could not have done any more. It's a shame he was sixth again, but he showed once more what a true fighter he is.

'When we saw him fighting for third we couldn't believe it because we were not sure if he could maintain the pace knowing how tough on tyres this track is. But he did keep his pace and that was impressive. His fight with Valentino was extra special and terrific to watch.

'Not too many guys get overtaken by Rossi and then pass him straight back. That, too, was incredible. It was a special show from James and we are really proud of him. He should be proud of himself. He gave himself a memorable birthday present with that ride.'

'He rides like a devil. He rides like his life is depending on it'

VALENTINO ROSSI

Pos	Pts	No	Rider	Nation	Team	Bike	Total time
1	25	1	Casey Stoner	AUS	Ducati Marlboro Team	Ducati	40'56.643
2	20	46	Valentino Rossi	ITA	Fiat Yamaha Team	Yamaha	41'03.147
3	16	69	Nicky Hayden	USA	Repsol Honda Team	Honda	41'03.848
4	13	48	Jorge Lorenzo	SPA	Fiat Yamaha Team	Yamaha	41'08.143
5	11	56	Shinya Nakano	JPN	San Carlo Honda Gresini	Honda	41'08.557
6	10	52	**James Toseland**	**GBR**	**Tech 3 Yamaha**	**Yamaha**	**41'08.886**
7	9	4	Andrea Dovizioso	ITA	JiR Team Scot MotoGP	Honda	41'09.423
8	8	5	Colin Edwards	USA	Tech 3 Yamaha	Yamaha	41'22.563
9	7	14	Randy de Puniet	FRA	LCR Honda MotoGP	Honda	41'22'680
10	6	64	Loris Capirossi	ITA	Rizla Suzuki MotoGP	Suzuki	41'23.442
11	5	24	Toni Elias	SPA	Alice Team	Ducati	41'23.670
12	4	13	Anthony West	AUS	Kawasaki Racing Team	Kawasaki	41'44.451
13	3	21	John Hopkins	USA	Kawasaki Racing Team	Kawasaki	41'44.976
14	2	50	Sylvain Guintoli	FRA	Alice Team	Ducati	41'45.542
15	1	7	Chris Vermeulen	AUS	Rizla Suzuki MotoGP	Suzuki	41'55.578
16		33	Marco Melandri	ITA	Ducati Marlboro Team	Ducati	42'08.410
Not finished first lap							
		15	Alex de Angelis	RSM	San Carlo Honda Gresini	Honda	
		2	Dani Pedrosa	SPA	Repsol Honda Team	Honda	

AUSTRALIA
ROUND 16

RESULTS

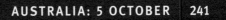

MALAYSIA

Sepang Circuit, 19 October

It all went horribly wrong in Sepang . . .
or should that be Se-prang?!

I was really looking forward to the race, buoyed up by my tangle with Rossi and the others in Australia

▼ Valentino and Nicky both had something to smile about after their performance at Sepang.

POLINI MALAYSIAN MOTORCYCLE
GRAND PRIX

Just when I thought it was all coming together for me after that great race in Australia, it all went horribly wrong in Sepang . . . or should that be Se-prang?!

It just goes to show that in this game, and especially at this level, you cannot take anything for granted.

I was really looking forward to the race, buoyed up by my tangle with Rossi and the others in Australia. My general feeling was that I could be on the pace and could mix it with the best of them when it came down to the hard riding stuff.

I had put in a lot of gym time, getting myself in perfect nick and building my stamina for what was going to be a sweltering outing in Malaysia. I knew what to expect, I had tested there earlier on in the year, and was pretty pleased with the way things had gone.

And despite some difficulties once again with the set-up, I managed to put in some not-too-bad laps and, for a brief spell, topped the timesheets in qualifying, when the track was still wet after a torrential downpour. But then it all went wrong as it dried out and, in the last ten minutes, I went swiftly backwards down the field and finished twelfth fastest. We got the timing wrong and left it too late to get the right setting.

After that it was downhill all the way – a real mess and a totally forgettable weekend and race.

Nothing really clicked for me and I got off to a lousy start and had to push really hard, right on the limit, to force my way through the field. It developed into a tough dog-fight with Anthony West and Randy de Puniet, as upfront Pedrosa, Rossi and Dovizioso left us all behind.

We'd raised the front end so the bike would steer a bit better – that had been a big problem. It had been giving me problems on the brakes and on the entry into corners, and it was messing me up big time.

Being where I was on the grid makes it had work and I got boxed in on the first corner. I braked later than everybody else around me, made up a couple of places, but ran wide and found myself in a real ding-dong.

I was running a harder front tyre to make the race distance and I think I needed one lap more to get it up to the right temperature. I paid the penalty for trying too hard to make up for the time and ground I had lost.

My downfall was turn seven on lap three. And down I went, thankfully without injuring anything, except my pride.

I had put in a lot of gym time, getting myself in perfect nick and building my stamina for what was going to be a sweltering outing in Malaysia

I got off to a lousy start and had to push really hard, right on the limit, to force my way through the field

There might not have been much shoulder-to-shoulder action going on upfront, but there was plenty of it where I was and I have to hold up my hands for some of the things that went on.

I had a close call, a touch, with Westy at the hairpin on lap two, and that was my fault – I plead guilty to that one. I thought I could out-brake him, but he was releasing his stoppers on the way in and I nearly T-boned him. There was contact, big time, and I was sure we were both going down. It was me who came off worst though, and I deserved to.

Then I had another close shave, this time with de Puniet, but nothing too serious. When I did eventually crash out it was because I was all fired up and pushing too hard.

I noted that West blamed me for wrecking his chances of beating his teammate Hopkins for the fifth time in six races – though he was pretty laid-back about the incident and didn't come storming into our garage.

He said: 'I had a chance to finish in front of John, until Toseland took me out. First, he took me out in turn one. I got past him again and then he T-boned me into the hairpin. He hit me pretty hard and I ran wide. I thought his riding was pretty loose.'

Fair enough . . .

It was a real disappointment not to have done much, much better in qualifying, and then to crash out so early in the race when all my instincts had told me I was in line for a good result to follow the success of Phillip Island. My confidence had been boosted in the morning warm-up when I had clocked the eighth fastest time without any undue effort. I knew I had the pace. What I didn't have was the luck and the opportunity to see it through.

Herve summed it up this way: 'James didn't get the start he wanted and he was pushing really hard, as ever, when he crashed.

'But if you don't do that and really try with some extra effort then you only follow people. And we don't want that. So while it is disappointing for us all, him in particular, he did go down fighting. And fighting hard.'

I have just got to put all that upset behind me as simply another bump on my learning curve, and go forward to the last race in Valencia with all the determination I can muster.

It is a circuit I am familiar with and I know my motivation will fire me up to finish my rookie season in MotoGP with a flourish at least as memorable as my all-out effort in Australia.

Pos	Pts	No	Rider	Nation	Team	Bike	Total time
1	25	46	Valentino Rossi	ITA	Fiat Yamaha Team	Yamaha	43'06.007
2	20	2	Dani Pedrosa	SPA	Repsol Honda Team	Honda	43'10.015
3	16	4	Andrea Dovizioso	ITA	JiR Team Scot MotoGP	Honda	43'14.543
4	13	69	Nicky Hayden	USA	Repsol Honda Team	Honda	43'14.865
5	11	56	Shinya Nakano	JPN	San Carlo Honda Gresini	Honda	43'16.590
6	10	1	Casey Stoner	AUS	Ducati Marlboro Team	Ducati	43'19.647
7	9	64	Loris Capirossi	ITA	Rizla Suzuki MotoGP	Suzuki	43'21.943
8	8	5	Colin Edwards	USA	Tech 3 Yamaha	Yamaha	43'24.809
9	7	7	Chris Vermeulen	AUS	Rizla Suzuki MotoGP	Suzuki	43'29.181
10	6	14	Randy de Puniet	FRA	LCR Honda MotoGP	Honda	43'31.523
11	5	21	John Hopkins	USA	Kawasaki Racing Team	Kawasaki	43'33.616
12	4	13	Anthony West	AUS	Kawasaki Racing Team	Kawasaki	43'47.406
13	3	50	Sylvain Guintoli	FRA	Alice Team	Ducati	43'51.624
14	2	15	Alex de Angelis	RSM	San Carlo Honda Gresini	Honda	43'55.010
15	1	24	Toni Elias	SPA	Alice Team	Ducati	44'05.146
16		33	Marco Melandri	ITA	Ducati Marlboro Team	Ducati	44'09.335
17		9	Nobuatsu Aoki	JPN	Rizla Suzuki MotoGP	Suzuki	44'54.370
			Not classified				
		48	Jorge Lorenzo	SPA	Fiat Yamaha Team	Yamaha	25'38.557
		52	**James Toseland**	GBR	**Tech 3 Yamaha**	**Yamaha**	4'19.122

MALAYSIA
ROUND 17

RESULTS

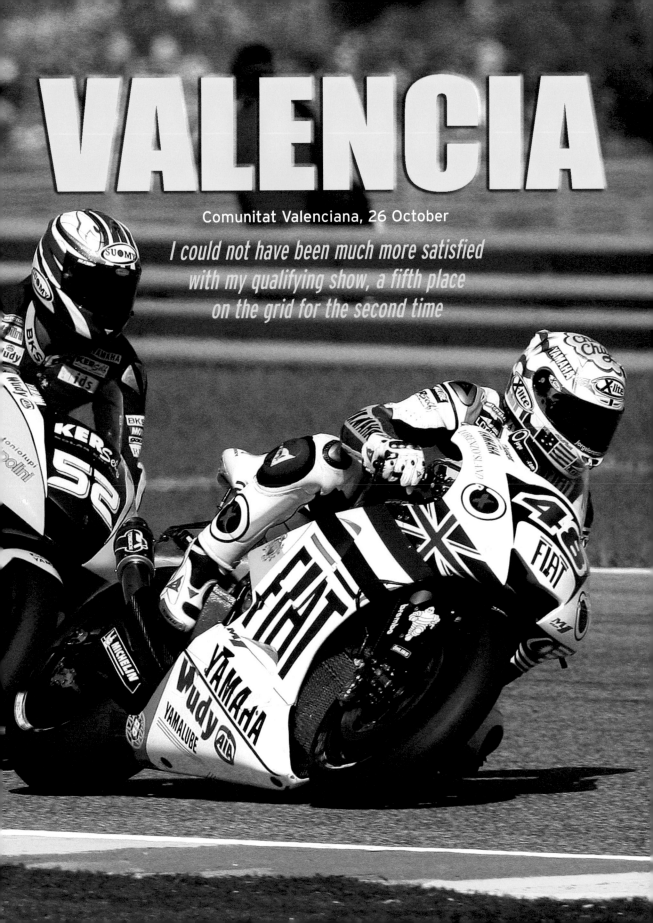

VALENCIA

Comunitat Valenciana, 26 October

*I could not have been much more satisfied
with my qualifying show, a fifth place
on the grid for the second time*

I had a really tough old tussle with Jorge Lorenzo for fifteen laps.
I got past him twice, only for him to get me back.

had already enjoyed four podiums at Valencia, the scene of the finale in this year's MotoGP season, in my World Superbike days. I knew and enjoyed the track, its atmosphere and its flowing layout, which is just the job for getting into a rhythm without sheer flat-out 200mph bursts. In short, it's a riders' circuit.

I could not have been much more satisfied with my qualifying show, a fifth place on the grid for the second time. It could well have been fourth if I had not been baulked by Marco Melandri. But sadly it all counted for sweet nothing when the lights went out for the start of the race, in front of 110,000 fans and in beautiful sunshine.

I got bogged down from the off and was very quickly engulfed in the rush away from the line. After that I had a really tough old tussle with Jorge Lorenzo for the next fifteen laps. I got past him twice, only for him to get me back.

On a purely personal note, even though my points helped the Tech 3 Yamaha team to clinch fourth place in the constructors' championship, it certainly was not how I had planned to finish my debut season in MotoGP.

I just about managed to hang on in there, even though I was under a lot of pressure as Stoner disappeared into the far distance and left a real midfield scrap behind him.

In the first half of the race I would say I was a bit quicker than Lorenzo but I just could not make it stick when I overtook him, and he's a real fighter so you know what to expect. At one stage, going into turn one, I put my hand up in the air to apologise for a move on him that was a tiny bit too close for comfort – and as I put it back on the bars for the second corner I missed my braking marker. And that was really annoying.

The usual old problem of fading grip came into play and in the closing stages I was struggling to hold onto what I had earned and still strive to fight off the bunch around me, even though I didn't have 100 per cent confidence. We had tried a big change in the set-up and, for a while, it worked well. But towards the end I was forced to ride defensively to make sure I did not drop too many places.

Having to fight hard for eleventh place is not my game plan when I know I am better than my record suggests. I'm convinced that, if it comes down to riding and racing hard, I can live with the best of them.

The last three laps were real nerve-tinglers and I had to give it my all, right on the edge, against Sylvain Guintoli, John Hopkins and Chris Vermeulen.

The last three laps were real nerve-tinglers and I had to give it my all, right on the edge, against Sylvain Guintoli, John Hopkins and Chris Vermeulen.

RESULTS

Pos	Pts	No	Rider	Nation	Team	Bike	Total time
1	25	1	Casey Stoner	AUS	Ducati Marlboro Team	Ducati	46'46.114
2	20	2	Dani Pedrosa	SPA	Repsol Honda Team	Honda	46'49.504
3	16	46	Valentino Rossi	ITA	Fiat Yamaha Team	Yamaha	46'58.308
4	13	4	Andrea Dovizioso	ITA	JiR Team Scot MotoGP	Honda	47'10.273
5	11	69	Nicky Hayden	USA	Repsol Honda Team	Honda	47'12.346
6	10	5	Colin Edwards	USA	Tech 3 Yamaha	Yamaha	47'18.323
7	9	56	Shinya Nakano	JPN	San Carlo Honda Gresini	Honda	47'20.685
8	8	48	Jorge Lorenzo	SPA	Fiat Yamaha Team	Yamaha	47'21.775
9	7	64	Loris Capirossi	ITA	Rizla Suzuki MotoGP	Suzuki	47'24.342
10	6	15	Alex de Angelis	RSM	San Carlo Honda Gresini	Honda	47'33.697
11	**5**	**52**	**James Toseland**	**GBR**	**Tech 3 Yamaha**	**Yamaha**	**47'38.221**
12	4	50	Sylvain Guintoli	FRA	Alice Team	Ducati	47'38.464
13	3	7	Chris Vermeulen	AUS	Rizla Suzuki MotoGP	Suzuki	47'38.947
14	2	21	John Hopkins	USA	Kawasaki Racing Team	Kawasaki	47'39.341
15	1	14	Randy de Puniet	FRA	LCR Honda MotoGP	Honda	47'39'525
16		33	Marco Melandri	ITA	Ducati Marlboro Team	Ducati	47'54.501
17		13	Anthony West	AUS	Kawasaki Racing Team	Kawasaki	47'57.295
		24	Toni Elias	SPA	Alice Team	Ducati	48'23.169

If Herve was disappointed that I had failed to convert my grid position into a bigger points haul he did a good job of disguising it, and said: 'Fourth place in the constructors' championship is a fantastic way for us to finish the season and I really want to thank both Colin and James for their efforts.

'In the end we beat two factory teams – and you cannot get much better than that. That was our target before this weekend and that is what we have achieved. We will be back before the end of November to start our preparations in Jerez for next year.'

I'll be putting all the lessons I have learned this year to good use in 2009 in the hope of making a big impression.

I can't wait!

CONCLUSION

Well, where did that year go? I suppose when you are enjoying yourself as much as I have been, despite the intermittent setbacks and heartbreaks, time just flies by.

I'll look back over my rookie season in MotoGP with a mixture of disappointment and delight, but also with growing excitement and anticipation for the future. I've gained some new and firm beliefs about my ability, and I now know that I made the right move when I switched from WSB, even though there could well have been more world titles to add to the two I won.

The challenge presented by MotoGP was irresistible and it was a feeling that never faded throughout 2008, whatever mishaps or setbacks sabotaged my hopes just when I honestly thought a podium was on the cards.

As much as anything, I have felt so much support from so many people – family, total strangers, loyal fans and workmates alike – that I have never been so down that I might have lost faith in what I could do on a motorbike.

The Yamaha Tech 3 team, headed by Herve, have been brilliant and their backing, sometimes in the direst of circumstances, has been an absolute joy and allowed me to give it my best shot whenever I raced. My manager Roger Burnett, too, has been a formidable ally, a sympathetic sounding board and an inspiration when I most needed it, like my awfully disappointing experience at the British Grand Prix.

And it has been fantastic to read the fans' emails, all of them uplifting and buzzing with encouragement, on my website. I am only sorry that I could not, for whatever reason, give them precisely what they and I most coveted . . . a win, or even a podium.

There were a couple of times when I honestly believed I could have been finishing in the top three, but if I take anything away with me from my first season it will be my showing in Australia, when I had one hell of a battle and mixed it with Valentino. That was like my coming of age in the top flight and it really underlined what I can do when the bike behaves and responds to my demands.

There have been some spats with other guys, all forgotten afterwards, due to my aggressive style – but that's the way I am and I don't moan if the tables are turned and I get muscled about in the touch-and-go melees. It is all part of the game. And, I must point out, there has never been a single word of caution, either officially or otherwise, from Paul Butler, the race director. He said he has seen nothing wrong in the way I have been riding.

What has pleased me is that, despite having to learn new tracks, find out what the bike would do, get used to a whole new back-up team and still battle with the best riders in the world, I have managed to hang on in there and crack some well-established MotoGP stars.

I have worked really hard at my fitness, listened as intently as I could to the advice of people like Herve and my super-friendly teammate Colin Edwards, and thread it all into my attitude.

I even bought a house close to the team HQ in the south of France so I could get to know the guys better and spend as much time as I could around the bike. My music has pretty much taken a backseat and I have not been able to do as many gigs with my band Crash as I have done in the past.

I think it will be the same in 2009, but one musical priority I have definitely committed to is to write a song for my mum's upcoming wedding. And I'll be singing her on her way to her honeymoon.

As for me, I've put the idea of any serious relationships on hold for now so that I can concentrate all my efforts and energies into making my mark in MotoGP. That is just one of the sacrifices I am willing to make in pursuit of my dream to be world champion, and follow my heroes like great Brits Mike Hailwood and Barry Sheene.

If I did not have this compulsion to be a winner, despite the obvious dangers, I could easily have turned my back on bikes and taken up the offer of a recording contract with Sony. Rock legends Status Quo even offered to play a backing track for me, and jazzman Jools Holland dragged me up on stage to play the piano at one of his concerts in front of 25,000 fans.

So much – good, bad and downright tragic – has happened to me throughout my life I feel I am well equipped to cope with whatever else, however dramatic, lies in store for me.

My aim to be a winner, and a champion, again is what keeps me going.

MotoGP CHAMPIONSHIP TABLE 2008

Pos	Rider	Nation	Team	Points
1	Valentino Rossi	ITA	Fiat Yamaha Team	373
2	Casey Stoner	AUS	Ducati Marlboro Team	280
3	Dani Pedrosa	SPA	Repsol Honda Team	249
4	Jorge Lorenzo	SPA	Fiat Yamaha Team	190
5	Andrea Dovizioso	ITA	JiR Team Scot MotoGP	174
6	Nicky Hayden	USA	Repsol Honda Team	155
7	Colin Edwards	USA	Tech 3 Yamaha	144
8	Chris Vermeulen	AUS	Rizla Suzuki MotoGP	128
9	Shinya Nakano	JPN	San Carlo Honda Gresini	126
10	Loris Capirossi	ITA	Rizla Suzuki MotoGP	118
11	**James Toseland**	**GBR**	**Tech 3 Yamaha**	**105**
12	Toni Elias	SPA	Alice Team	92
13	Sylvain Guintoli	FRA	Alice Team	67
14	Alex de Angelis	RSM	San Carlo Honda Gresini	63
15	Randy de Puniet	FRA	LCR Honda MotoGP	61
16	John Hopkins	USA	Kawasaki Racing Team	57
17	Marco Melandri	ITA	Ducati Marlboro Team	51
18	Anthony West	AUS	Kawasaki Racing Team	50
19	Ben Spies	USA	Rizla Suzuki MotoGP	20
20	Jamie Hacking	USA	Kawasaki Racing Team	5
21	Tadayuki Okada	JPN	Repsol Honda Team	2

ACKNOWLEDGEMENTS

Thanks to Herve Poncharal and all the crew at Tech 3; Yamaha for giving me the chance to ride in MotoGP; and last but by no means least, the British public for their unrivalled support.